Walter Baumann · Marcel Werren
COW PARADE

COWPARADE

Zurich's lighter Side

text: Walter Baumann
photography: Marcel Werren

NEPTUN

© Copyright 1998 by
NEPTUN VERLAG AG, Postfach, CH-8280 Kreuzlingen

Text: Walter Baumann, CH-8602 Wangen

Photography: Marcel Werren, Fotostudio Obrist & Werren,
CH-8005 Zürich

Jacket Design: Marcel Werren, Fotostudio Obrist & Werren,
CH-8005 Zürich

Design, Setting:
Logotype, R. Kaufmann, CH-8272 Ermatingen

Translated from the German by Michelle Durham Bastianello

ISBN 3-85250-108-1

Josef Estermann
Mayor of Zurich

Who would have ever thought that the city of Zurich would turn into one big Alpine pasture in the summer of 1998? Even the most die-hard of urban cowboys could have never dreamed of this. Yet, just ten years ago Zurich was taken by storm when packs of freshly painted lions invaded the downtown, turning the Bahnhofstrasse overnight into one gigantic color-filled savannah. And now, to the ringing of bells, a colossal herd of cows has arrived by boat at Bürkliplatz, wandering out into the city pastures, where they are certain to be grazing the whole Alpine summer long.

What a prospect! These decorative cows are drawing in thousands from near and far who don't want to miss a chance to see this unique cattle show.

They won't be disappointed, either. Figuratively speaking, Switzerland's richest pastures lay at their feet this summer as there's nothing one can't find among the flower-filled meadows of downtown Zurich.

Many thanks must be extended to the City Association for bringing us this Alpine procession of a very special kind, one which has turned Zurich's summer of '98 into a real feast for the eyes. There couldn't be a better accompaniment to the given occasion than this "cow-guide". May it serve you well this summer, as you take a stroll through the countryside of our city.

INTRODUCTION

Zurich's "Cow Parade", initiated by the Zurich City Association (an umbrella organization of Zurich retailers with over 1500 affilliated members), and documented by NEPTUN VERLAG, actually came about quite spontaneously. Exactly for this reason, most of the general public has had no idea how much brain and muscle power went into bringing these colorful cows out onto the streets. And yet, there was hardly any branch of this city's many-sided economy that didn't quickly and enthusiastically step forward to take part. The enormous wave of public interest has certainly attested to this successful mix of tradition, creativity and artistic ability. In fact, the event has grown out beyond the city borders, out to Kloten Airport – the city's "gate to the world" – and even as far as over the Gotthard Pass, into Ticino, where a couple of cows have managed to promote their homestead back up north. Naturally, this book can't cover in complete detail all of the 815 cows which have taken part in this "Cow Parade". Rather, we have left it to the photographers and writers to document the event through their own observations. One thing is certain, though – a unique picture book about Zurich has emerged.

We hope you enjoy this colorful "Cow Parade".

The Publishers

Opening, May 28, 1998: Boarding of the cows, Alpine procession along the Bahnhofstrasse at Pelikanplatz.

A STROLL THROUGH THE TOWN

GARY BROWN

Scottish-born interior architect of the CFP Gastro AG, is simply funny by nature. Hence, his very merry "Hiking Cow". Brown is also the creator of the Crazy Cow Restaurant interiors, and in addition, all of the cartoons for the "Verrückten Kuh" (Crazy Cow).

For Edith Strub, director of Zurich Tourism, this cow event is a welcome adjustment to Zurich's stiff business image.

Every Wednesday and Saturday, Zurich Tourism is inviting tourists on an entertaining stroll among the cows. The walk begins with the leading cow, "Crazy Cow". Guides direct visitors to the prettiest, most original and funny cows. The walk ends in the restaurant "Crazy Cow", Hotel Leoneck, on Leonhardstrasse 1, where strollers can taste a bit of "Brännti Crème" (a sweet dessert).

right page, locations of the painted cows.

P

P

P

Stadelhofen

P

P

Rämistrasse

P

Seilergraben

P

Bellevue

Altstadt

Zürichsee

Limmat

Limmatquai

Bürkliplatz

Central

Schipfe

P

Limmat

Bahnhofstr.

Oerlikon

Storchengasse

Schaffhauserplatz

Rennweg

Bahnhofstr.

Paradeplatz

Schanzengraben

Flughafen

Hauptbahnhof

P

Shopville

Bahnhofstr.

P

Löwenstrasse

Löwenplatz

P

Letzipark

P

Löwenstrasse

Pelikanstrasse

P

Sihl

Stauffacher

JÜRG BÄCHTOLD

describing his work: "Impressions of nature form the basis of my paintings. I use different materials like old sheet metal, fabric, filler, and paint (acrylic) to create compositions. Out of these various applications of materials, reliefs evolve, creating a three-dimensional effect. The shadows cast by the different structures is an integral part of the composition, also adding to the color and form. I prefer the square format, whose strictness and neutrality, I believe, are an essential part of the painting."
In addition to three other cow-designs, he also created the 26 "Trachtenmädchen" (girls dressed in traditional costume), as well as the 6 trade cows for the carousel on Paradeplatz. From 1957 to 1962, he studied to be a graphic designer at the Kunstgewerbeschule in Zurich. Since 1958, he has been artistically active as a painter, exhibiting throughout Switzerland.

Zurich Main Station, the largest and most important of the seven train stations located in the city, truly embodies Swiss Railway history. It was one hundred years ago, on August 9, 1846, that Nordbahn's first train made its way from here to the famous health resort in Baden in the canton of Aargau.

This precursor to what is now the SBB, (Swiss Federal Railways), was then called the "Spanish-brötlibahn" (Spanish Pastry Railways). It derived its name from the fact that, most often on weekends, its trains would transport a Baden breakfast pastry specialty to the city of Zurich. The small train station, in those days located outside the city limits, stood back behind a picket fence out in the middle of a pasture.

The Zurich Tourism Association has taken the Zurich Retailers' "Cow Parade" as an opportunity to symbolize that which began with the start of the railway system – tourism – in the form of three cows: the city stroller with his camera slung over his shoulder ready to go; the world traveler schooled in proper etiquette; and the businessman with a flair for commerce and communication. The cows have been designed by Jürg Bächtold.

Sketch of the "Business-Kuh" (Business Cow) by Jürg Bächtold

ALL THE WAY TO THE TOP

PARTICIPANTS:

Gschwend-Gastrobau
for Bern-Lötschberg-Simplon-Bahn

Sculptura
for Braunwaldbahnen AG

Luigi Grendene
for Celeriner Bergbahnen

Antonio Cauanini
for Intercontainer-Interfrigo

Alex Zwahlen
for Riederalp-Bahnen Aletsch

Primarschule Vitznau
for Rigi-Bahnen

Ursina Battaglia
for Rothorn Bahnen Schweiz

Pfuschi (H. Pfister)
for Selecta

Hansjörg Lutz
for Sersa

Hauser und Gilardoni
for Sportbahnen Elm

Zurich's spirit, and that of its international influx of visiting friends, is as mobile as a mobile. Indeed, it has been this active spirit and continuous innovation that has made Zurich what it is today – the little global city located along the Limmat river; a Swiss metropolis of trade, art, press and science.

The larger-than-life mobile now hanging in the newly renovated, true to the original, main hall of the train station, is a wonderful representation of the teamwork between the government and canton railways, between the private railways, as well as the mountain railways and shipping companies. The cows dangle lively between artist Niki de Saint Phalle's gigantic angel and artist Mario Merz's neon numbers. The Elmer cow, (Elm is a mountain resort in canton Glarus), might remind some of the "Martinsloch", a gigantic hole in the Glarner Alps through which, twice a year, at the end of September and beginning of October, the sun casts its morning rays onto the church steeple in the town of Elm.

The "Elmer Kuh" created by Glarus artists, Tina Hauser and Silvia Gilardoni.

HIGH TECH

**MOBILE
COMPONENTS:**

Crossbars:
fiber glass tubes, diameter:
75, 90, 100 mm,
span: 4 and 6 m.

Fastenings:
steel 80/8 and 120/8 mm,
M16 galvanized screws.

Cables:
stainless steel cable 8mm, ball-
bearings
rotation blocks, various connectors.

Cows:
fiber glass/polyester mixture
ca. 35 kg.

Locomotives:
plywood, 36 kg.

Weight:
total load 3 x 360 kg.

Width:
maximum possible width 33.5 m.

Highest point of suspension:
19 m above the floor.

This large mobile consists of three independently moving smaller mobiles, each of which holds 5 hanging objects. All connection points turn in a 360 degree radius. The crossbars can be precisely adjusted to the differing weights of the objects. All fastenings are removable so that differing combinations can be created or individual mobiles can be hung separately.

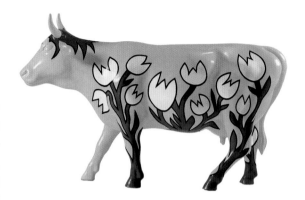

OPEN ON SUNDAYS

ANDI LUZI

was born in Chur, Switzerland on September 3, 1958, and spent his childhood in Neuhausen am Rhein-fall. Following a period of apprenticeship and then travels, he turned his attention in 1988 to an autodidactic study of fine arts. During 1995/96, he moved back and forth between Neuhausen and New York. Since 1997, he has been living and working in Neuhausen, Berlin and Polen. Wall and room murals are the artist's trademark. And so it was that he was put in charge of painting all of the rooms and the entry foyer of the Carlton Arms Hotel in New York. Andi Luzi has exhibited his work in well-known galleries at home and abroad.

Shopville – this was the winning title in a competition to name the big underground shopping arcade located beneath the main train station. An international word to reflect an international city. Today, escalators run from every side of the station down into the largest shopping center in Zurich, which houses store upon store deep below the square on which the statue of the Swiss Railway System's engaged promoter of Alfred Escher stands.

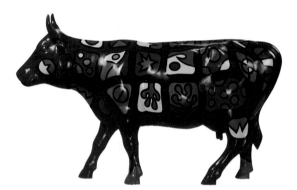

The life of the artist who designed the cows has been as international as the mix of languages that awaits one down in Shopville. In the past few years, the work of the self-educated artist has spread across most of northern Switzerland and also into Holland, Bavaria, Poland and New York, and of course, Zurich. This coming summer, Andi Luzi will celebrate his 4oth birthday.One more reason to raise a glass of milk to his amazing fantasy and creativity . . .

A total of 40 cows currently populate the shopping center located under and next to the railway tracks. Shopville houses 128 stores, of which a dozen or so are restaurants.

SPRAY PAINTERS CAUGHT IN THE ACT

Participants in the Spray Painting Contest:

Auf der Mauer Isabelle,
8045 Zürich, «Käse»

Beer Romeo,
8302 Kloten, «La vache protectrice»

Bollinger Peter,
8810 Horgen, «Karos»

Eisele Susi ,
9014 St. Gallen, «Romantic»

Graf Ruedi,
8045 Zürich, «Sein oder Design»

Hodel Sabine,
8967 Widen, «no Milk»

Huber Markus,
8707 Uetikon, «Fisch»

Iliadis Andy,
8048 Zürich, «Urwald»

Jucker Trix/Bühler Judith,
8484 Weisslingen, «Kids»

Krieg Susanne,
8824 Schönenberg, «Regenbogen»

Lukas Ernst,
8038 Zürich, ohne Titel

Meier Stephan,
8050 Zürich, «Fische»

Michalopoulos George,
8003 Zürich, «Faces»

Neely Christopher,
8032 Zürich , «Silhouette»

Pernod Nana,
8008 Zürich, «Kiss»

Pfiffner Daniela,
8634 Hombrechtikon, «Pop Art»

Pfluger Monique,
8134 Adliswil, «Jugendstil»

Romanillos Angel,
8806 Bäch, «Hinterteile»

Schmid Jan,
8046 Zürich «Pop Art»

Stapfer Désirée,
8103 Weiningen, «Lovely Cow»

Widmer Andreas,
8427 Rorbas, «Spiel»

Idee, Konzept, Realisation,
EBSQU,
E. + B. Seeberger-Quin, 8005 Zürich

"Spray a cow and become famous!" was the title and motto of the public competition organized by the Renters Association Center Main Station. Of the 200 submitted designs, 21 were selected, and their designers invited to a 3-day live spray-painting event in Shopville.

George Michalopoulos's "Faces" won 1st prize, a trip to New York; 2nd prize winner, Markus Huber's "Fisch", won a 2-hour shopping spree through Shopville; and 3rd prize went to Sabine Hodel for her "no Milk", which won her a 1-hour shopping spree through Shopville.

2nd Price: won by Markus Huber.

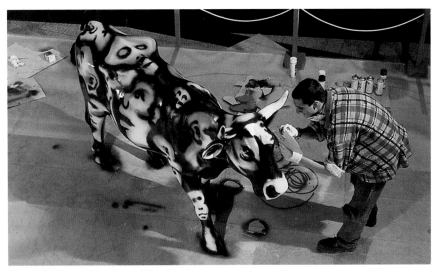

Winner of the competition: George Michalopoulos

BON APPÉTIT

MAGDA BLAU

who resides in Merlischachen, has been a painter for over 30 years. Recently, her work has expanded into textile design and ceramic painting – she has contributed to Langenthal Ceramic Factory's line of limited art editions. The "Sternen-kuh" (Star Cow), the "Velofahrerin" (Bike Rider) on Limmatquai, and the cow from Kurt Widmayer, all carry her trademark.

KARIN SCHAUB

Zurich, decorated the "Au Premier" cow.

Bahnhof-Buffet Zürich HB
Restaurant "Stars"
location: Hauptbahnhof

right page,
Restaurant "Au Premier"
location: Hauptbahnhof.

It's a totally new experience in dining, to say the least, coming face to face with the supplier of your dinner as she gently looks out at you from under thick lashes. It doesn't seem to bother her, though. She just stands there waiting patiently on what will be better times.

ARRIVING AT THE STATION

PETER KLICK

internationally renowned interior architect, has brought the idea of "wanting to break free" literally into action.

MARLIES ZÜRCHER

Atelier DEFACTO, Zurich, unmistakably designed this doorwoman. Andrea Brenner, Zurich, painted it.

With the opening of the new train station in October 1871, what was then the largest free-span hall in Europe, Zurich was elevated to a modern tourist city. The whole city was invited to its opening. And what did they most admire about the new train station? According to newspaper reports, it was the "elegance of the restrooms".

A whole row of hotels stood across from the train station at this time. Everything from the "National-Terminus" to the "Victoria" to Mr. Habisreutinger's "Habis Royal". The English stayed at the "Victoria", out of respect to their Queen. The Germans and Scandinavians preferred the "Schweizerhof", a hotel name which could be found from the Rhine Falls to Interlaken and Luzern. In Zurich, the first "Schweizerhof" was located on the Limmatquai, but later moved to the Bahnhofstrasse to be with most of the other (first class) hotels, where it soon played a dominant role. In keeping with its reputation as one of today's most prominent high-class hotels, it has presented its cow in perfect likeness: a hotel doorman donned in red livery and cap, a lapel shining with two silver keys. In a similar manner, many at this summer's event have tastefully represented themselves without being too overt with pushy advertising. For many, it was simply their love for Zurich which led them to take part with pleasure and enthusiasm in this spirited cow-festival.

Interhome, location: Bahnhofplatz 7.
right page, Hotel Schweizerhof, location: Bahnhofplatz 7.

COW HORNS

PETER BISCHOFBERGER

Hüttwilen, Estermann & Partner, Tägerschen, designed the "Jägerin" (the Huntress).

ALAIN AND VERENA BLANK

reside in Thun. Alain Blank was born in Lausanne in 1961. He attended design school in Basle and then in Zurich, were he received his degree in 1987. Since that time, he has been working as an artist, and as a professor at the Schule für Gestaltung Zürich, and since 1993, as a teacher at the Ecole cantonale d'art de Lausanne, as well. His work can be seen this year (1998) in an exhibition of his work in the Kunstmuseum Thun. "Durchbruch und Ausblick aufs Land" (Breakthrough to and View of the Country Side), is a collaborative piece of the Blanks.

Cow horns, which produce a very powerful sound, are known as the oldest wind instruments and alarms. They were later duplicated in brass. They once served as battle horns in times of war, and were also used by firefighters, later by stage coach drivers and eventually by track inspectors on the first railways. The horn represented pride and modernity. For this reason, it was used by many of Zurich's residents on their houses and for their family coat of arms. For instance, there was the "Schwarze Horn" (Black Horn) on Rüdenplatz, the "Gelbe Horn" (Yellow Horn) on the Grauen Gasse in the "Oberdorf" and the "Gelbe Hörnli" (Little Yellow Horn) in the "Niederdorf". A closer look at the tavern sign to the guild house, "Zur Schmiden", on the corner of Marktgasse and Rindermarkt, reveals a tiny gold-plated horn which recalls the original name of the house, "Goldenes Horn" (Golden Horn), first written reference dating back to 1373.

Albrecht-Schläpfer AG, location: Lintheschergasse / Schweizergasse.

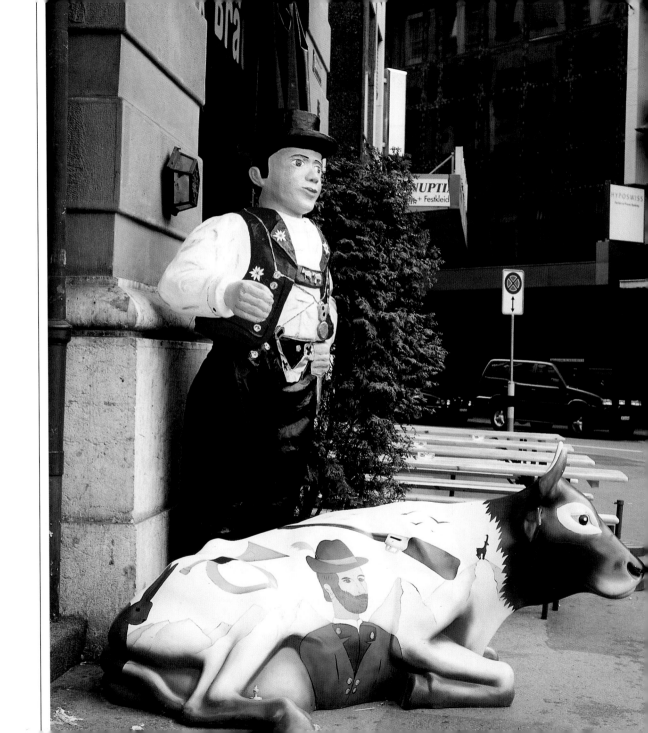

Restaurant Du Nord
location: Bahnhofplatz.

THE SHOWCASE OF SWITZERLAND

24

**DENIS
EYER-OGGIER**

Naters, has her skiers promoting
the winter fun to follow in Obergoms.

HELMUT KOCH

St. Gallen, self-employed artist with
his own atelier for painting and
object design, has bestowed his
"Harley" cow with wings, enabling
her to take off at any time, if need
be. By the way, gourmets shouldn't
pass up this: evenings in his
restaurant "Helvetia", this creator
of 3-dimensional objects spoils his
guests with a five-course meal.

The soon to be 140 years old Bahnhofstrasse is the
boulevard of Zurich. There are probably over 50
streets that go by the same name in Switzerland,
and certainly over a thousand in all of Europe, but
Zurich's is the only world-famous among them. It is
known as the showcase of Switzerland, a street
lined with prominent businesses and shops, filled
with a variety that can't be seen anywhere else, the
perfect place to take a stroll. It was actually out of
this street that Zurich developed into the tiny cosmopolitan city that it is today. Originally planned as
the link between the train station and shipping traffic on the Lake of Zurich, Fröschengrabenstrasse,
later renamed Bahnhofstrasse, was the first shopping street, from which everything sprung up. It was
here that the Gotthard train was planned as the
European North-Sourth connection, and the first
street car junction was developed. It was on what
later became the Bahnhofstrasse that the first
department stores were erected. And just recently,
it was here or to be more exact, on the neighboring
historic Löwenstrasse, that the City Association
came up with the first ideas about what eventually
came to be this summer's "Cow Parade". It is certainly not meant to be earth-shaking, this event, but
rather intends to show just how little it really takes
to spread joy and draw so many in to the fun.

Albrecht-Schläpfer AG, Location: Lintheschergasse / Schweizergasse.

Verkehrsverein Obergoms
Location: Bahnhofstrasse 89/91.

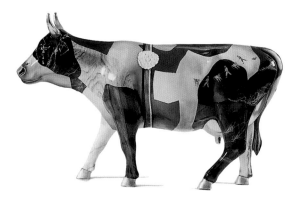

The teamwork of students and teachers at the educational center,
SMGV, shows the variety and wealth of craftsmanship of the painter's
profession. Location: Pestalozziwiese / Bahnhofstrasse.

DANI AMBÜHL

Zurich Gallery Owner, converted Radio 24 and Tele Zürich into a cow.

SALVATORE MAINARDI

was born in Italy in 1954, and has been living and working for 21 years in Spreitenbach where he has his own atelier. In Salerno, he attended an art school, already taking part in an art exhibition at the young age of 16. Cryptically, and with humor and sensitivity, the artist draws out the surreal by linking the world of the unconscious to everyday life. Take a closer look at his "Sexy Girl".

"Sexy Girl", left, Mondo Valentino, right Radio 24 / Tele Zürich, Location: Bahnhofplatz near the Linthescher fountains.

COSMOPOLITAN

Kuoni Reisen AG, location: Bahnhofstrasse / Bahnhofplatz 7.

GERHARD MÜLLER

born in 1956, illustrator, lives and works in his own atelier in Dietikon. Alongside of advertising graphics, he designs fair backdrops, creates murals for indoor swimming pools and restaurants, and also designs cars. He has exhibited in Lucerne, Dietikon, and in the Canary Islands. In addition to the "Ohr" (Ear), he also designed cows for Welti Furrer, as well as his own. (see pp. 35, 116/118).

KATY GURTNER-MURPHY

mother, housewife and "all-arounder", she was born in Evansville, Indiana in 1951, and lives today in Meilen. After attending Stanford University, she went half way around the world to end up here. The artist does book illustrations, oil paintings, watercolor and acrylic, typography and calligraphy. She managed to cover a cow with a lot of brain work.

THE KUONI DISPLAY DEPARTMENT

created enticing vacation destination points all around the world, from underwater adventures to the Safari, just about to the moon!

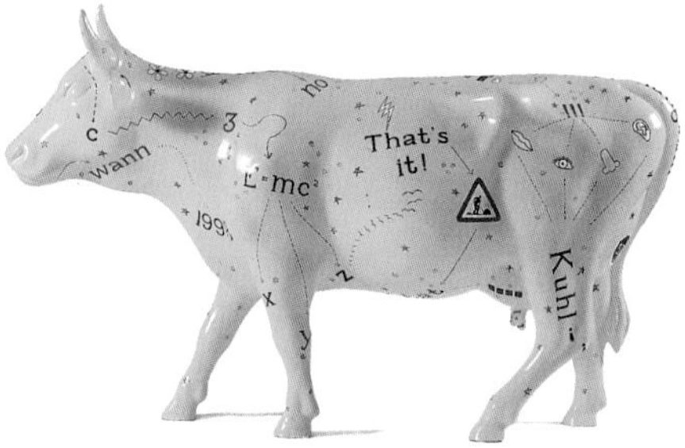

"Rent a Brain", location: Bahnhofstrasse 106.

MICRO-ELECTRIC HÖRGERÄTE AG, Zug, location: Schweizergasse 10.

Kuoni Reisen AG, location: Bahnhofstrasse/Bahnhofplatz 7.

SO THE SAYING GOES...

BENNY FASNACHT

lives and works in Basle. His "Bell Kuh" comes to us direct from the Alps, well-nourished from the finest of herbs.

HEIRI SOLLBERGER

residence in Zurich, shows with the precision of a butcher, where to locate the best pieces of the cow. For Messer Dolmetsch, he designed three other cows: two are standing in Shopville and a third on Limmatquai 126.

Holy Cow! A total of fourteen separate entries are listed under the words, "Chue, Chüeli" (Cows, Calves) in the 1983 edition of the "Zürichdeutsche Wörterbuch". Just to mention a few:

That fits like a cow in a mouse hole.
(doesn't fit)

She understands as much about housekeeping as a cow does about dancing.
(doesn't understand anything)

To do the cow.
(clown around)

All cows were once calves.
(everyone was inexperienced at one time)

He's a calf.
(not reasonable)

Cow nails
(frostbite on the tips of the fingers and toes)

Cow deal
(shady business)

Messer Dolmetsch, location: Bahnhofstrasse 92.

BELL AG, location: Bahnhofstrasse 102.

SPACE DREAM

THE MANOR DISPLAY TEAM

took a unique "outer space" view of the city – their five cows show the approach and landing of a band of martians.

"The cow is a banal animal, good-natured but simple-minded, useful but cumbersome, harmless and humorless. And because of this, it is easy to make so much out of them and with them," says the very well-meaning Sonntagspresse. The management of the City Association are delighted by the support and involvement of the media. According to the Swiss maxim:

Be Art great or be it small
Artists have the respect of us all.

Manor AG
location: Bahnhofstrasse 75.

SPORTS BUFFS

HEINZ BLUM

originally from Basle, graduated as a graphic designer. He married in Paris and has lived in Zurich since 1967. He created his first mural for an event 25 years ago, and in the meantime over 130 have come to be admired in Switzerland, Germany and other countries. Naturally, Blum – what else would a Basler do? – has painted many "Fasnacht" carnival lanterns. Large blank canvases have never held him back, and he certainly never misses the opportunity to slip in a bit of humor, here and there. His central aim in painting is to express nature, harmony and the joy of life.

Other cows designed by Heinz Blum can be seen at Hotel Adler on Rosengasse 10, Hotel Du Thèâtre on Seilergraben 69 and Hotel Rigihof on Universitätsstrasse 101. In addition, four ELVIA-cows on Bleicherweg 19, on the Clariden-strasse 41, on the Dörflistrasse 120 and on the Lavaterstrasse 83.

Four pairs of top-fit cows currently graze the walk-way out front of a well-known insurance company on Bahnhofstrasse. They proudly display Switzerland's great enthusiasm for sports: from Hornussen (a traditional farmers sport) to jogging, to cross-country skiing and ice skating, one "ZSC" member, (Zurich's ice skating club), ready to go, hockey sticks and all.

The Zurich artist Heinz Blum, creator of over 100 murals, has given the impression to those who take a closer look, that these milk-makers really do seem to be enjoying their moment in the sports limelight.

EIVIA Versicherungen
location: Bahnhofstrasse 89.

EXCITEMENT IN THE AIR!

ARTHUR BERINI

born in 1960, has worked in Zurich since 1981 as a painter, creating as well posters, space designs, murals, glass mosaics and multi-media concepts. The classic Cashmere pattern, which embodies many symbols such as the tree of life, also elegantly suits lady-like cows.

FELDPAUSCH DISPLAY TEAM

These cows are certainly in full bloom!

GRADIMIR SMUDJA

born in Yugoslawia, 1956, studied painting and graphic design at the Belgrad Art Academy. He has been living in Toscana since 1994, where he has painted what have become significant works of art. He also devotes time to the design of textiles. His most cherished theme is the paraphrasing of old masters, which he has certainly succeeded in doing with Van Gogh's sunflowers… onto the contours of a cow, no less!

Goldschmidt Ilimod AG
location: Bahnhofstrasse 65.

right page
Feldpausch
location: Bahnhofstrasse 88.

What's behind all this cattle business? Is that just pure advertisement plastered to the contours of those Zurich cows? In anticipation of this summer's event, over 400 firms, among them out-of-towners, made sure to reserve a cow for themselves, some going as far as to claim a dozen. And each has offered its own unique take on the event. There have been a few ornery onlookers complaining that what they see is certainly not art, but that it was never intended to be. What is it all about, then? Well, just take a look at how interesting, lively and talked about Zurich has become – there's excitement in the air!

Madame Damenmoden, location: Bahnhofstrasse 63.

«FREIE LIMMAT!»

CARLA SCHENA

and the display team from Globus, turned the arcade alongside the department store into an African wilderness, wonderfully populated by Savannah natives. At the same time, the artist has emphasized the current trend this summer – the safari-look.

PETER SAUTER

and his team from Atelier Fabritastika, Brüttisellen, conceptualized and created this glockenspiel. To the amusement of both young and old, with just the push of a button, six cow bells chime out five different tunes from "Old McDonald had a farm", to "Oh, Susanna" to the Swiss traditional, "Chumm mir wei go Chrieseli gwünne" (Come, let's go harvest cheeries!).

Snapshots from the Globus Zoo.

"Freie Limmat" was the slogan heard shortly following World War II, the perhaps these days regrettable demand to demolish the "Unteren Mühlesteg" (Lower Mill Bridge), which due to this fervent call for freedom, was approved in a public vote. Along with it went the "gedeckte Brüggli" (Covered Little Bridge), too. Today's Globus Department Store, which stood at this time on the former Werdinselchen (then an island in the Limmat), was forced to move to Löwenstrasse, to a lot upon which the Linth-Escher-Schulhaus had stood until then. What is of urban interest is the green located directly in front of it, which extends out to the Bahnhofstrasse. During the parceling of the lots along both sides of the planned Bahnhofstrasse, it was exactly this little piece of land that found no interested buyers. Who, in those days, wanted to buy the "Sihlwiesli", which up to 1865 was the location for the guillotine? The city was left with no other choice but to furnish the chic Bahnhofstrasse with a quaint green. What better place today for a fiber glass cow?

An additional note of interest– in October 1899, only a few weeks before his death, the Höngger philanthropist and art dealer, Caspar Appenzeller, donated the soon to be one hundred year old Pestalozzi Monument to this grassy spot, to this day a much-admired and often-photographed statue.

ANGELA BANDELLI

Oberrohrdorf, created the funky cow for D. Peterhans.

ERNST HIESTAND + PARTNER AG

Studio for Design Consulting, Visual Design, Zollikerberg, in collaboration with

PETER OSWALD

Tann, created the ice-cold Eiger mountain range

KATHY MOSER

Atelier DEFACTO, acted as make-up artist.

GERHARD MÜLLER

Dietikon, born in 1956. The main portion of his work lies in illustrations, back-drop designs for fairs, and air-brush painted murals for indoor swimming pools and restaurants. His cow is the sexy "Straps-Diva" (Garter Diva).

Eiger (Europe) AG (left)
Marbert AG (right),
location: Pestalozziwiese.

right photo,
David Peterhans, Oberrohrdorf (left),
Gerhard Müller (right),
location: Pestalozziwiese.

Glockenspiel McDonalds, location: Pestalozziwiese.

HISTORICAL PRESERVATION

GERTRUD ARPAGAUS

Art Director of Bernie's Display Department, along with her whole team, have taken Noah's Ark to depict the cow's role in our lives and our survival.

BRIGITTE FORRER

Display Department Bogorad, created this fanciful linen costume. Tailored by S. Peccora.

SILVANA JÖRG

Kloten, born in 1966, populated Löwenplatz with these forest animals.

Genossenschaft Migros (lower bottom left and right as well as in the background right, artist's portrait see pp. 38/39), Herren Globus, (background left) location: Löwenplatz.

At one time, the big-city like Löwenstrasse led to the 17th century erected city fortress, the Löwenbollwerk. In 1884, it received a new addition with the opening of the Moorish Synagogue of the Israeli religious community. The cantonal historical preservation society once fought against a planned demolition of this building as this old Zurcher Synagogue was one of the few remaining Jewish cultural buildings in Europe that did not fall victim to the anti-Semitism of the 1930s. "Besides, this building is an impressive example of the once popular application of the oriental form in synagogues."

left, Herren Globus, location: Löwenplatz.

bottom left, Leinenhaus Bogorad & Co., location: Usteristrasse 17/Löwenplatz.

Bernie's, location: Löwenplatz.

MIGROS MOOSEUM

Paul Klee
by Sandra Picenoni ①
Keith Haring
by Marcel Spiess ②
Franz Kline
by Cécile Hoffmann ③
Christo
by Regula Tschabold ④
Ferdinand Hodler
by Jean-Pierre Weber ⑤
Andy Warhol
by Antonio Lonoce ⑥
Max Bill
by Urs Isler ⑦
Hundertwasser
by Denise Hauser ⑧
Hans Arp
by Armin Eugster ⑨
René Magritte
by Maria Mazzillo ⑩
Joan Mirò
by Larissa Bonorand ⑪
Piet Mondrian
by Regula Tschabold ⑫
Wilhelm Busch
by Maria Mazzillo ⑬
Niki de Saint Phalle
by Dina Xandry ⑭
Joan Mirò
by Thomas Choi ⑮
Jackson Pollack
by Cécile Hoffmann ⑯
Daim by Marcel Spiess ⑰

The group of apprentices in the Migros Display Department have taken twenty cows and painted each in the style of a famous artist. The public will now have the chance to take part in a competition to guess which cow belongs to which artist. The cows are currently being displayed in front of Migros City on Löwenstrasse and on Löwenplatz. They will later be auctioned off and the money donated to charity.

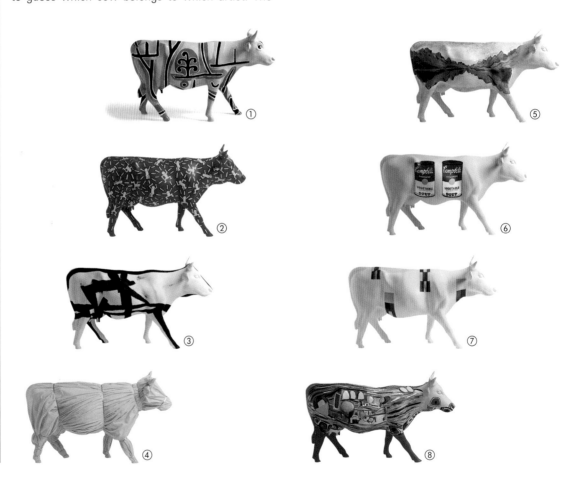

Three cows were unfortunately banished from this Mooseum, due to objections raised by Pro Literis:

Roy Liechtenstein
by Natascha Matthys

Pablo Picasso
by Jeanette Müller

Roy Liechtenstein
by Tanja Tarolli

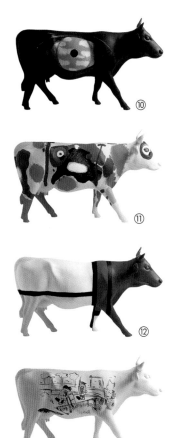

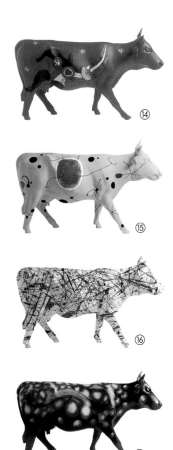

RICH IN CONTRAST

HANS PETER GILG

Art Selection, Zurich, calls his two cows "Kuhwiese" (Cow Meadow) and "Kuhglocke" (Cow Bells). The bells are not just ornamental – a ringing mechanism has been built into the inside of the cow.

CHRISTINA BAUMANN

has set the "Kuh-tisch" (Cow Table) with a red and white check table-cloth. The artist lives in Zurich.

SEREINA FEUERSTEIN-BUCHER

residence in Zurich, painted her cow in pastel check.

Between the two medieval branches of the Sihl river, which at one time flowed into the Limmat at the old Schützenhaus directly in front of the city wall, once stood the Family Werdmüller Sawing Mill, built in the 14th century. But following the incorporation of Aussersihl into the city on January 1, 1893, the mill and the neighboring "Oetenbachhügel" were seen as taking up space which could better be used to accommodate traffic. And so, in 1902, the mill was demolished and they began to dig through the hill, in order to pave way for the Ura-niastrasse. This street received its name from the observatory, a 45 meter high tower, which the city architect, Gull, built for a private company in 1907. On the southeast corner of the tower, Gull established the Werdmühlplatz. On the longer sides, he built a bank and a governmental building with storefronts below at street level. Today, the plaza is only open on one side to traffic, and is nonetheless a calm oasis from the otherwise hectic bustle of the inner city.

Kitch'n' cook AG, location: Werdmühleplatz.

right page, CREDIT SUISSE, location: Werdmühleplatz.

CHAGALL AND NAPOLEON

GÜNTHER ALEXANDER

born in 1946, lives in Arni where he works in his own Atelier for Design and Display Window Decoration. His Chagall-inspired cow appears so light and full of bounce.

Hausmann AG
location: Urania-Strasse 11.

CHRISTOPH STEINEMANN

STONEMAN, was born in Basle in 1968 and lives today in Ennetbaden. He studied painting and sculpture at the San Francisco Art Institute and received his degree from the Kunstgewerbeschule Zürich in display design. His work has been exhibited both at home and abroad.

Speaking of Napoleon, one has to wonder how that cow will ever manage to bring its hand to its chest. STONEMANN also created three striking cows for the Rennweg Stores Association, see pp. 45/46, as well as the "Waser-Kühe" on Limmatquai.

Brasserie Lipp
location: Urania-Strasse 9.

THIRST-QUENCHERS

MARGOT FREI

resides in Zurich and teaches display design at the Allgemeinen Berufsschule ABSZ. In contrast to this city's certainly ever-visible and omnipresent construction sites of the civil engineering department, her idea to have a simple cow grazing in the carved out excavation of a foundation puts the emphasis on getting back to nature. It is in fitting with the development of Rennweg into a traffic-free zone, and the therefore long return of nature back into the city.

There are about 1200 public fountains in Zurich. Originally, the city's fountains were named after, or depicted, saints and biblical figures. This was done in order to protect the water from being polluted. During the Reformation, though, these names and depictions were replaced by classical figures and names out of the Greek, Roman and German mythologies. This is how Zurich came to receive the name, "Limmat-Athen". The "Hercules" fountain, which replaced the former Rennweg gate, originally stood on the other side of the street, in front of today's Jelmoli Department Store. And it was at the start of the Neumarkt that "Jupiter" once stood. The goddess "Juno" still stands to this day on Paradeplatz. The first written reference to the "Hercules" dates back to 1732. It is regarded as the most beautiful and striking of them all.

Civil Engineering Department of Zurich
location: Herkulesbrunnen/Herkulesplatz.

DARCO KNEZEVIC/ PHILIP KÒSER

have been working as artists for about a year and half now, mainly in the Baden region. They have created 11 cows for Franz Carl Weber, including "Globi" (cartoon figure), who celebrates his 60th birthday this year. In addition, they designed two cows for the Bahnhof Apotheke and the black and white spotted cow for the hair salon, Coiffure Black & White.

CHRISTOPH STEINEMANN

shows everything the Rennweg stores have to offer. Artist's portrait, see p. 43.

left
Franz Carl Weber AG
location: Herkulesbrunnen/Herkulesplatz

below
Rennweg Stores Association
location: Herkulesbrunnen/Herkulesplatz.

THE COW DOCTOR

VITUS ALBERTIN

born in 1954, currently resides in Dürnten, where he has his own atelier. He creates abstract paintings. His work has been shown in various exhibitions both at home and abroad.

HELENA MUSIL

Decoration Atelier of the Confiserie Feller AG, lives in Dürnten.

In collaboration, they have deliciously created the "Spiegelei" (Fried Egg) and "Cassata-Glace" (Cassata Ice Cream). Gran Café on Limmatquai 66.

Unfortunately, as was the case 12 years ago during the Lion Festival, this summers events have not been free from vandalism. Already before the official opening, vandals had maliciously destroyed some of the cows — horns were ripped off, heads torn, stomachs and backs scratched. As a result of this bad experience, though, this year's event organizers have come prepared with an expert repair service which is not likely to be out of work any time soon.

Confiserie Feller, La Cafette
location: Herkulesplatz.

right page
Rennweg Stores Association
location: Rennweg.

ALONG THE "ÖDEN BACH"

ELSO SCHIAVO

born 1934, painter and graphic designer, lives in Baar, and works in Baar and Zurich. Since 1975, his work has been shown in exhibitions both at home and abroad. The art commissions range from paintings to murals, space design, sculpture, lithography and textile design. He is the creator of the foulards and ties worn by the CH-Olympic Team in Lillehammer. And he was the top-prize winner in the International Stamp Competition in Japan (1990).

His cows are happy cows, and cheeky, too, at least the ones for the Schweizer Tierschutz STS (Swiss Animal Protection) (location: General Guisan-Quai) and for the Enge-Apotheke (see pp. 130/131).

ERICH BERNEGGER

from Zurich, painter, and André Hoinkes from the Tanzschule Sonja created the striking zebra.

Zurich's well-known Oetenbachgasse originally got its name from the "öden Bach" (barren creek), which once flowed out into the lake at the Zurihorn. And it was out along this river bank that Zurich's first group of nuns decided to build a modest cloister for themselves. But after continual flooding, these ladies thought better and moved themselves into the city where they built what became Zurich's largest nun cloister on the "Sihlhubel", near the Lindenhof. Change of address didn't mean change of name, though, as the nuns went right on calling it "Oetenbachkloster". Today, the Oetenbachgasse is a quiet little alley way. Its greatest attraction now is Zurich's largest sewing shop offering a broad selection in buttons. One such button, award-winning in the U.S, is actually used today as the store's logo — it is a button of a button, so to speak. The artist used such logo buttons to decorate the cow.

Tanzschule Sonja. location: Rennweg.

sketch by Elso Schiavo

right page, Peter Keck AG, location: Rennweg/Oetenbachgasse.

GRAZING COWS

VRENI BOLLIGER

lives and works in Männedorf. She was educated as a fashion illustrator, but has been a self-employed illustrator for over 13 years. She mainly does fashion illustrations and children's books illustrations… but she also enjoys spraying cars! She has managed to realize a very original concept – a pasture running along the facade of a building.

Domestic Cattle (Bos taurus). Family: Horned Ruminant.

Two types of wild cattle lived among our most ancient ancestors: the bison and the auroch. The domestic cow evolved out of descendants of the aurochs, which over time spread over a large expanse of the earth.

Cattle (calves, cows, bulls, oxen) are plant-eaters. They feed off of the plants in pastures, the hay produced from these plants, clover, carrots, potatoes and everything else the fields have to offer. These animals flourish when they are able to spend the warmer months out in the pastures.

In order to get the necessary quantity of food, the cow roams the fields feeding slowly for hours at a time. Its strong legs and hooves make this possible. Its long neck makes it easy to reach the ground, while its extremely strong neck muscles enable the animal to keep its head bent for hours at a time.

Cattle are highly valued for of the milk they supply us. A well-nourished cow, which is not used for labor, can produce between 7–10 liters* a day. Its milk contains all of the substances necessary to human nourishment, especially a child's. Among the various breeds, the spotted and brown cows have come to be most valued. Of the spotted cows, which

flourish well in hilly regions, the yellow-white Simmental cows are most widely bred due to their large milk supply.

*Today, an average of 30 liters according to Toni-Milchzentrale!

"Grasende Kühe" (Grassy Cows), Vegi-Restaurant Hiltl
location: corner of Uraniastrasse / Sihlstrasse 28.

ANDRÉ
TIEFENTHALER

Zurich, born 1960. After studying
display design, he apprenticed with
DRS to become a stage designer.
As Art Director of Jelmoli Department Store, he has designed a
whole herd of cows, from spotted
ones to woolly ones, even some
never-before-seen, like the
"cow-raffes" and "zebras".

Jelmoli
location: covered entrance,
Bahnhofstrasse / Seidengasse.

Christ
location: entrance Jelmoli,
Bahnhofstrasse / Seidengasse.

right page
true to the original spotted cows,
Jelmoli, location: Bahnhofstrasse /
Seidengasse.

«WHERE ARE THE COWS?»

The Atelier of

**A. BERNINI/
P. PELLANDA**

Zurich, painted the whole Jelmoli Herd. The "Wäscherin "(the Laundress) and the detailed design of the spotted cows are the work of Peter Pellanda. See p. 32 for Arthur Berini's portrait.

**LAURENT
SPIELMANN**

1967, Fribourg, Display Department, Christ, devotes his free time to painting and to building architectural models. His cow is black and white, of course, because he is from Fribourg, (whose cows are black and white, as well as the canton's flag).

Jelmoli
location: Bahnhofstrasse / Seidengasse.

called out the Japanese tourist as he stepped out of the bus at Bahnhofstrasse. Andreas Zürcher, Director of the City Association, bursts out laughing when he recalls this moment. What better proof of the success of this event?

The City Association have heard from other European cities wishing to possibly do the same. The Mayor of Nicosia wants to do something similar with the Mufflon, a cypriot wild sheep. Some organizers of a film festival would like to ship a cow all the way to Hong Kong! The editorial page of the Zürcher Zeitung has certainly given voice to a fair share of critics, some of whom have referred to the event as "pseudo-ethno-stupidity", "plastic monsters", "virtual crap". Organizational Committee President Rico Bisagno is actually happy about the response: "The fact that these gentle animals have affected people certainly has to do with the archetypal aspect of the cow. It has always been a symbol of comfort and beauty…".

DISPLAY TEAM BUCHERER

were inspired by Dali. This cow covered in real cow fur carries surreal traces, and is lined in a plethora of Dali clocks.

Bucherer AG
location: Bahnhofstrasse 50.

WONDERFUL PREDICTIONS

56

ROLF HÜRLIMANN

Stafa, born in Zurich in 1954, is a
gallery owner and painter. His
figurative oil paintings are mainly
inspired by Venice. He can always
be found there at the annual carnival and at regattas. His cows, the
"Zünfterin" (Guilder) and the
"Orchidee" (Orchid) have a touch
of Venice to them.

MANFRED
SCHNEEBERGER

(1957–1998), Display Designer for
Bally on Bahnhofstrasse 66, from
1986–1998, conceptualized the
splendid "Schühlein" (Little Shoe).
It was made by the Display Team at
Bally (Schweiz) AG in Schönenwerd.

Confiserie Teuscher
location: Bahnhofstrasse 46.

Bally (Schweiz) AG
location: Bahnhofstrasse 66
Bahnhofstrasse 32, Uraniastrasse 10.

At the opening of festivities, Mayor Josef Estermann humorously welcomed the procession of cows
when he referred to them as a fitting symbol for this
land of milk and honey. In addition, he expressed his
hopes that the seven lean years just behind us
would now finally be followed by seven fat years.
"Let's show this recession our horns!"

KUHSCHWEIZER

HEIKE WANNER

born in 1971, lives in Vienna. Following school, she worked as an apprentice to a gold smith. She has won a number of prizes in professional competitions, placing first in a competition while still an apprentice. Since 1996, she has been self-employed in Vienna, and has founded a workshop with three other artists called, "STOSS IN DEN HIMMEL" (Push into Heaven). She has also taken the Master Craftsman course for gold- and silversmiths and jewellers.

Everything good comes from above: The angels seem to be watching over the very international Credit Suisse Bank, whose cow is covered in a global map lit up with little red lights indicating the bank's branches world-wide.

"Kuhschweizer!" This is what the Swabian people north of the Rhine called the Swiss, when they were accused of paying their bills with fake money during a shooting competition in 1458, in Constance. This ended up being no little matter as it sparked a war against Swabia, Germany. All of this is ancient history, now. It is no longer an insult to remind Zurich of its rural past – and this summer, the city streets certainly attest to this!

CREDIT SUISSE
location: Bahnhofstrasse 53.

HANS RUDOLF WEBER

born in Chur in 1935, lives and works in Forch where he has his own atelier. Early on, it was landscapes that fascinated the artist, while today it is abstract painting. His paintings can be viewed in well-known Swiss galleries. Since 1996, he has exhibited designs, steles and sculptures in his own gallery. "Blue Nancy" and "Red Folly" are the names of his cows. He has selected the color red to represent love, intimacy, and human essence. Blue is a symbol for joy, freedom, the endless blue of the sky and universe.

In Hans Rudolf Weber's work, the form is a way of expressing joy, humor and the ever-returning "Clin d'oeil".

"Blue Nancy" and "Red Folly" by Hans Rudolf Weber, location: CREDIT SUISSE, teller hall, Bahnhofstrasse 53.

"GSUND UND FRISCH"

PAUL LEBER

Zurich, designed the Coop cow, "Gsund und frisch" (Healthy and Fresh). Artist portrait, see p. 105.

LILIANE SCHLUMPF

Display Department St. Annahof, lives in Zurich. She is the creative designer of the mountain cow, "Edelweiss" and the playful "Zwerglikuh" (Miniature Cow).

"Gsund und Frisch" (healthy and fresh) – so the motto goes at Zurich's largest and oldest grocery store, St. Annahof Coop, on the Bahnhofstrasse. Just the Annahof-Alpine-procession, alone, is made up of 10 uniquely designed cows, each as pretty as the leading cow. Here, the cows feel quite at home because one of Coop's artists also designed the now world-famous Christmas lighting hanging along the Bahnhofstrasse.

"Healthy und fresh Cow" from Paul Leber, location: Coop Stadelhofen.

St. Annahof, location: Bahnhofstrasse 57.

TATJANA GLENSER

Display Department St. Annahof, Zurich, created the beloved, "Marienkäfer" (Ladybug). She also designed "Superman".

MAGIE JANSEN

Display Department St. Annahof, Zurich. Her "Cowfrau" is young and fresh, a western gal in blue jeans, cowboy boots, suspenders and all! Not to forget the colt, of course.

ELISABETH MÜLLER

Display Department St. Annahof, Zurich, is the creator of the clown, "Die dumme Augustine" (can be compared to a female rendition of Bozo the Clown).

St. Annahof
location: Füssli-Strasse.

MILK'S GOOD FOR YOU

KUNDRY

was born in 1946 and raised in Steiermark. Already as a teenager, she taught classes in verre églomisé technique, and received her first commission to do a wall mosaic. In Constance, she established her own atelier. In 1986, she married the Thurgauer landscape painter, Hans Niederhauser. Since 1980, she has been self-employed. Her work is composed of poetic photo realism, still lifes, and landscapes, symbolic and surrealistic watercolors, lithographs, stainedglass and sculpture.

HANS NIEDERHAUSER

born June 8, 1930, he has lived with his wife, Kundry, since 1976 in Fruthwilen. The painter, Hermann Knecht was his mentor. Since 1976, he has been a self-employed artist running his own painting school, "Malen am Bodensee". He has exhibited his work both at home and abroad in individual and group exhibitions. Since 1995, his work, and that of his wife, have been shown in a permanent exhibition in their own gallery in Kreuzlingen. His art encompasses landscape paintings in oil, wood-cuts, stainglass windows, sculptures and fountains.

The Talacker quarter is regarded as the finest in the city, and the intersection of Talackerstrasse and Pelikanstrasse, in the shape of a rhombus, has always been endearingly referred to as "das Plätzli" (the little plaza). With subtle irony, Gottfried Keller, the renowned Swiss poet, praised this noble district inhabited by newly wealthy silk barons, home to not one tavern or any other trade and whose streets were cleaner and whiter than any other in Zurich. And still today, this area stands out from the rest as a slice of yesteryear's idyllic among the hustle and bustle of this now modern city of commerce. The people here are fond of remembering the fact that Gottfried Keller once inhabited this quaint neighborhood. It is on this baroque plaza which the Thurgauer Milk Industry has chosen to display its magnificent cows. Decorated in rural scenery, one finds, among other things, an authentic traditional Thurgauer maiden.

Ostschweizer Milchproduzenten
(Milk Association of Thurgau,
St. Galler-Appenzeller Milk
Association, Säntis AG), location:
Pelikanplatz.

PAINTING IS THIS BUTCHER'S PASSION

LE BOUCHER CORPAATO

His civil name is Jean-Pierre Corpataux. Born 1950 in Freiburg. i.Ue. Trained as butcher and cook, 1973 recipient of the Master Butcher's Diploma. Corpaato has been painting meat since 1984, in order to give a behind the scenes look at how things are prepared.

He signs his paintings with the year "./."- The minus sign indicates Corpaato's way of counting backwards from the year 2000, in order to better prepare for the third millennium. Numerous exhibitions of his work can be found among other places, in London, Paris, Buenos Aires, Alabama, Vienna, Chicago, World Fair exhibition in Seville.

J.P. Corpaato designed not only the cows on Pelikanplatz, but also one for Blum Juwelier (p.70), two for Galerie Ernst Hohl, (p.82), one for Caveau Mövenpick and also one for Metzgerei Ziegler, (p.150).

On Pelikanplatz, eleven cows carry the trademark of Le Boucher Corpaato. As this painting butcher likes to clown around, he has accommodated the little painted polyester cows with a stabley, appropriately furnished with hay, of course. Out of bleached plastic has evolved quite a unique herd of cattle. "I have fallen eternally in love with the eyes of the "Kaufleuten" cow," pines Carpaato. Nevertheless, "Miss Simmental" remains his favorite. Without any reservation, she exposes her innermost self — juicy chops, tripe and tenderloins. Everything guaranteed BSE-free.

Interessensgemeinschaft Talacker / Pelikanstrasse / Sihlporte
location: Pelikanplatz.

COWRAFFES AND CROCOWDILES

HEIDI KÄLIN

Rüti, came up with the original idea of painting the fish in Zurich's lake. The idea was selected by 37 employees out of a total of 74.

ENRICO CASPARI

Zuberwangen, translated the idea onto the painted cow.

MALER SCHAUB

Zurich, designed the "Bauerin" (The Lady Worker).

HESCO Pilgersteg AG, Rüti, location: Pelikanplatz.

right page, Locher AG, location: Pelikanplatz 5.

As early as April 22, under the headline, "Kuhraffe und Krokuhdil" (Cowraffes and Crocowdiles), the Zürichsee-Zeitung brought us a humorous preview of things to come: "What 12 years ago the plastic lions were, soon will be the cows – a special attraction, and at the summer's end, objects to be auctioned off for Zurich's downtown. The city is going all out with a whole herd of polyester ruminants. Some are currently being prepared in Männedorf and Uetikon for their "Alpaufzug" (alpine procession), to be followed by their auctioning off in September. We hope for good summer weather for the sake of all participants, cows included."

NOMEN EST OMEN

LE BOUCHER CORPAATO

Fribourg, created the cow for Blum Juwelier. Additional cows by Corpaato, see p. 66/67, p.82, p. 150.

TED SCAPA

lives in Château Vallamand. The Swiss artist was born in 1946 in Amsterdam. He graduated from the Royal Academy in the Hague in graphic design. He worked abroad as a cartoonist for many years, in America, India and Hong Kong. In 1963, he came back to Switzerland for good, where he worked as director of an art book publishing company for over 30 years. For over 20 years, he was the moderator for the t.v. show, "DAS SPIELHAUS". His work has received various international prizes.

Up to 1850, when all of Zurich's streets and alleyways were given names and houses numbered, homes were distinguished by their names. In addition to visually descriptive names like, "zum roten Dach" (the Red Roof) or "am Thor" (at the Gate), animal names, as proud and exotic as possible, were especially popular – from deer to bears to elephants and peacocks; from storks to ravens and eagles. Amazingly, though, not once was "cow" ever picked from this whole zoo of animals. Obviously, the most useful creature of all, one as commonplace as dogs and cats, was so ordinary that it simply wasn't found suitable as a name for a house. It was different with the ox, though, which was mainly used as a symbol for butcher shops. The "Rote Ochsen" (Red Ox) was located on Weinplatz, the "Schwarze Ochsen" (the Black Ox) on Rennweg, and a well-known guest house established in the 15th century, "Zum Ochsen" (the Ox), was located on the outskirts of the city on the Sihl. An exception was the "Rote (also blutige) Rind" (Red (bloody) Cow) on the Weggengasse, later named "Zum Kind" (the Child), although not to be confused with the nearby restaurant, "Kindli"(Little Child), originally called "Christus-Kindli"(Christ Child), and today the "Opus".

Wohnbedarf AG, location: Talstrasse 11/15.

Blum Juwelier, location: Talstrasse 70.

Deutsche Zentrale für Tourismus DZT
location: Talstrassse 62.

ZURICH'S PANORAMA

CORDULA HUBER

illustrator and artist, was born in 1964 in Zurich, and presently lives here. After attending a teacher training college, she completed the pre-course at the Kunstgewerbe-schule Zürich, where she went on to study graphic design. In San Francisco at the Academy of Art College and at the San Francisco Art Institute, she went on to receive her Masters of Fine Arts. She did her practical training by GGK in Dusseldorf. In San Francisco, she worked as a freelance artist in the area of sign painting, murals, graphic design and illustration.

Since 1994, she has been working in Zurich as a self-employed artist, illustrator and graphic designer doing work for, among others, Weltwoche, Sonntagszeitung, NZZ-Folio, Bilanz, Annabelle, Spick, Bonus, Bolero, Greenpeace. In addition, she is an art teacher. Cordula Huber's work, for which she has received some awards, has been exhibited in the U.S., in Hungary and in Zurich in both museums and galleries.

UBS has gone to town for this summer's festivities — a whole row of 10 cows currently graces its entrance. The recent successful merger of two of Switzerland's largest banks into the biggest financial institute in Switzerland with branches world wide, has certainly given the world something to talk and write about of late. In honor of the events, all of their picturesque cows have been created by just one artist. After a start in Zurich, this young artist went on to make a name for herself internationally, mainly in the US, as an illustrator and art educator. For this summer's event, she has chosen to dress UBS's cows in none other than fantastic Zurich panorama.

Just imagine, you are sitting in a boat out on the lake. You marvel at the city panorama around the hour. This is exactly what this artist did. In ten sections, she has transposed the subtle changes of day into night onto the body of ten cows.

UBS, location: Bahnhofstrasse 45. The "midnight cow" and its counterpart, the "midday cow", each display the Quaibrücke on one side, and on the other, the lakeside and Alps, in contrasting tones of day and night.

Midnight 12:00 am. front: Quaibrücke
back: lakeside to the right, Alps
location: Bahnhofstrasse 45

Morning 2:24 am. front: Bellevue
back: Zürichhorn, Alps
location: Flughafen, Terminal A

Morning 4:48 am. front: Opernhaus, lakeside,
back: Seefeld
location: Shopville

Morning 7:12 am. front: Seefeld
back: Opernhaus, Seefeld
location: Shopville

Morning 9:36 am. front: Zürihorn, Alpen
back: Bellevue
location: Bellevue

Midday 12:00 p.m. front: right lakeside, Alps,
back: Quaibrücke
location: Bahnhofstrasse 45

Afternoon 2:24 p.m. front: Mythenquai,
Uetliberg, back: Bürkliplatz
location: Airport, Terminal A

Afternoon 4:48 p.m. front: Uetliberg
back: Kirche Enge
location: Bleicherweg

Evening 7:12 p.m. front: Kirche Enge
back: Uetliberg
location: Oerlikon

Night 9:36 pm. front: Bürkliplatz
back: Mythenquai, Uetliberg
location: Flughafen, Terminal A

LISA

SYLVIA BÜHLER

born in 1963, lives with her family in Herisau. She was educated as a medical doctor's assistant. Her artistic career began in 1986 with the manufacturing of the very successful "Sascha" dolls, followed by hand-made figures. With these figures, she achieved gold, silver and bronze in international competitions. In 1994, she discovered painting on silk. Her paintings are figurative as well as abstract, with such elements as flowers, animals, cities, rituals. Her "St. Gallerin" depicts both city and countryside, symbolizing the way fabric was originally woven and embroidered in the country, and then brought to the city to be processed. The very graphic and fashionable edelweiss symbolizes the fashion styl Sturzenegger AG. The artist also made the cow covered in St. Galler embroidery and an "Appenzellerin" (A Woman from Appenzell) for Lehner AG.

HEIKO CORNELSEN

display designer for Michael Jordi SA, Nyon, created the Ethno-Cow. Globally encompassed, she still manages to keep her feet firmly planted in Switzerland's soil.

Cow names were originally most often inspired by the color of fur, whether it was brown or black or spotted... although, the form and placement of the horns also played a role. In the 19th century, people's first names started to find their way more and more into the stables; in fact, often times they were identical to the names of owners' children. The results of a 1952 cattle statistic showed that 82% of all cows had a feminine name.

And what about the glass-fiber born Zurich city-cow? "Lisa" is her name, and its a fitting one, having been derived from the first letters in the German title for this summer's event, "Land in Sicht Aktion".

Michel Jordi SA, location: Bahnhofstrasse 48/Augustinergasse.

right page
"Edelweiss" and "St. Gallerin" Ed. Sturzenegger AG, St. Gallen
location: Bahnhofstrasse 48/Augustinerstrasse.

THE PEARL OF OLD TOWN ZURICH

URS ROOS

graphic designer and illustrator,
was born on March 10, 1944 in Rapperswil. Following his education in graphic design, he worked in Denmark, Canada and Zurich. Since 1980, he has been running his own graphic atelier together with Ursula Roos. He currently lives in Niederweningen.

One hundred years ago, Strehlgasse, probably the oldest alleyway in Zurich, which at one time descended down from the Lindenhof into the old Roman harbor and thermal baths, was seen as so narrow and shabby that it should be torn down. But due to such strong protests, coming mainly from the at that time still very newly established Board of Historical Preservation, it was decided otherwise.

Today, this picturesque old town alleyway is full of fluctuating facade lines, which create a unique ambiance among the dozen or so select shops and boutiques selling the finest in jewelry, watches, lingerie, and antiques. Of exceptional note is the cultured pearl jeweler's shop, whose high-quality and broad selection can presently be found displayed along the imaginary catwalk, as such, of some of the our visiting four-legged friends.

THE BUTCHERS' FOUNTAIN

RAFFAEL BENAZZI

resident of Zurich, created this simple but effective composition.

One of Zurich's oldest fountains, erected in 1430 by the later mayor, Rudolf Stüssi, was mainly built to serve butchers, who required a lot of water for their work, and who were also forced, due to their "unclean trade", to work here on the Rennweg, along the outskirts of the inhabited neighborhood. This first fountain stood directly across the street from the butcher's guild house, "Zum Widder". Today, reopened as a chic hotel, it enjoys a centuries-old solidarity of tradition, which it has expressed in its own way at this summer's festivities – a white ram bathes in the fountain, cooling off from the summer heat.

Hotel Widder, location: Widder fountain, Münzplatz.

THE BELL RINGER

PAUL CARTIER

born in 1928 in Zurich, lives today in Richterswil. After studying at the Grande Chaumière in Paris, he has gone on to produce an extraordinary amount of work in his creative career, leaning toward the abstract and its fascinating suggestive effects which the figurative cannot always explain. This very independent artist does not let himself be swayed by trends, and has developed his own individual style. These two cows are unmistakably Cartier's. They recall his paintings, the round intersecting shapes and the symbolic colors: white for milk, yellow for cheese.

SUSI KRAMER

Oberhof. She became very famous through her object designs – paintings encased in acrylic glass – through the visa card, through the presence of her work in art exhibitions both at home and abroad. She has now started to paint her decorative patterns on vertically rectangular paper instead of canvas. The garden from Oberhofen, night and day, seasons and encounters of love are caught in a pure picturesque atmosphere. The "Künstlerkuh" (Artist Cow) designed by Kramer, revels in a sea of colors.

Glockengasse, located just about right in the center of the so-called "minderen Stadt" (poorer part of town) on the left bank of the river, first came to this name in 1790, and it was thanks to the wrong reasons – the classically designed house no. 9 "Zur Glocke" (The Bell), all the way at the top of the hill, is said to have once been home to St. Peter's bell ringer, and later the neighboring house to the St. Peter's Church Minister, J.C. Lavater, and his young friend J.W. Goethe. Yet, there is plenty of doubt as to whether it really did derive it's name from this legendary bell ringer. Records show that the bell-founder family Gloggner lived here in the "Glocke": Rudolf (1384), Albrecht and Johannes (1392) and, the Henslis, both father and son (1406). They wrote what became known as the famous "Gloggner Chronik", the most impressive account of the Battle at Sempach. Today, this peaceful alleyway, which leads up from the Strehlgasse, has become quite an insider's culinary hot spot.

"Das Pendent" from Boutique Façonnable.
Location: Nüschelerstrasse 1.

right page
Restaurant Barometer, location: Glockengasse 9.

"Künstlerkuh – in homage to Susi Kramer", location: Stüssihofstatt.

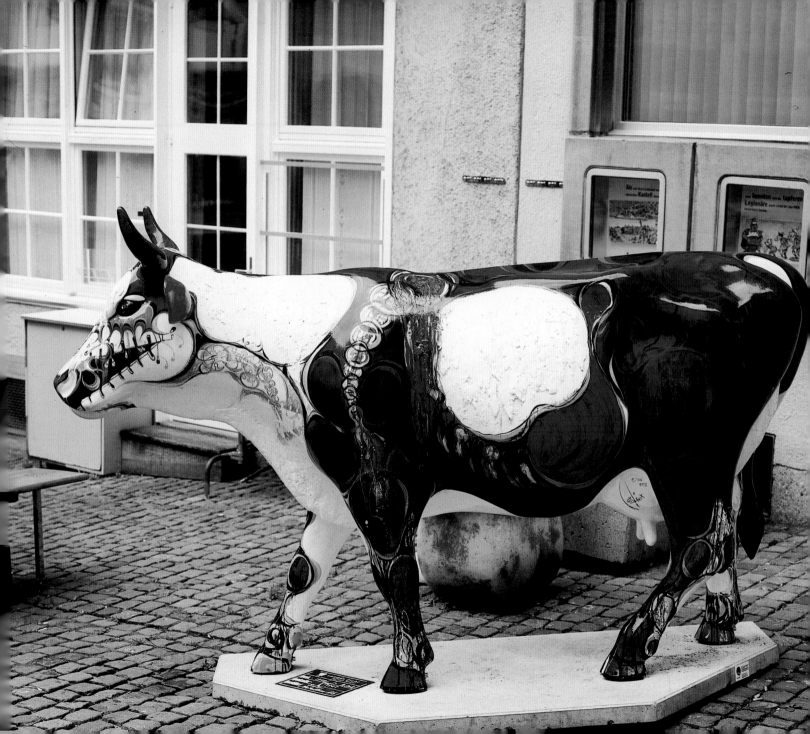

LOOKING GOOD

VLADIMIR AGUILAR

born in 1960, studied architecture and currently lives in Zurich. Today, his work mainly en compasser in interior architecture. He has designed display windows for Fogal stores world-wide. With his colorful "Beinmode" he brings color into the mundane gray of the everyday.

ALEX ZWAHLEN

born in 1958, attended art school in London. He lives and works as a self-employed artist in Zurich. His painted work has been shown in various exhibitions. Using collage and paint, he has managed to capture the "Meister-Käferlein" (Meister-Bug – this store's emblem) long enough to decorate this cow. The "Fabergé-Ei" (Faberge Egg) (p.89), the Riederalp-Bahnen Mobile-Kuh (Mobile Cow), as well as the locomotives (p.13), the Meister-Silber cows on Paradeplatz, and the cow at the ASIA Coffee Shop, Flughafen Zürich, are all his designs.

FOGAL
location: Bahnhofstrasse 38.

Meister Juwelier AG
location: Bahnhofstrasse 33.

In the company of banks, watch-, sports-, toy- and department stores, the latest in international fashion can be found prominently displayed along the boulevard, this summer most aptly celebrated out front of Bahnhofstrasse 38 by the "Beinmode Zentrale F.", an elegant cow representing the best in elegant, attractive, fine-quality hosiery.

COWS IN ART

OLD AND NEW PERSPECTIVES

Hans Schweizer – Untitled (1995)
Gouache on paper, 64 x 50 cm
Privately owned. Photograph:
Michael Rast, St. Gallen

Johann Hautle – Life on the Alps
(1996) Oil on painting board, 28 x 39
cm . Privately owned. Photograph:
Ernst Hohl, Zurich / Urnäsch

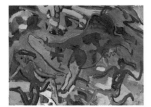

Bendicht Friedli – The Figures from
Nolde. Acrylic, 50 x 70 cm
Photograph: Foto Schenk, Unterseen

The arrival of the cow in art began not too far from here, in Zurich-Riesbach on the lake. The Zurich painter Rudolf Koller (1828–1905) studied in Belgium, France and Germany. And only first in 1850, in Munich, did he finally turn to depicting animals in art. In 1856, he built himself an atelier out on the Zurihorn, and added stables. He then bought himself a small herd of cattle, and proceeded to paint them from every possible angle. And so it was that he came to be a multiple award-winning master at depicting animals in art. Such paintings as "Kühe am See" (Cows on the Lake) (1862), "Mädchen mit Rind" (Girl with Cow) (1866), "Herde am Abend" (Herd in the Evening) (1867), "Viehherde" (Herd of Cows) (1870) and "Vieh auf der Alp" (Herd on the Alps) (1880) have become world famous.

In his showrooms on the Peterstr. 16, under the theme "Die Kuh gibt keine Ruh" (The Cow Won't Keep Quiet), Ernst Hohl is currently displaying a modern depiction of the cow in art.

Galerie Ernst Hohl, location: St. Peterstrasse 16
Two cows by Le Boucher Corpaato currently stand outside the entrance of the gallery. In addition, his paintings are being shown in the exhibition space inside. Artist portrait, see p. 66, Pelikanplatz.

DAVIDE PIZZIGONI

lives in Milan. A well-known theater costume designer, he has created all of the ties and foulards for Bulgari, as well as all of the firms advertisement.

This Italian artist was interested in the Greek origins of the Bulgari family, whose story begins in the middle of the last century in a small Greek town, Eparus. He has let his cow, who recalls the bronze antique sculptures, be inspired by Greek mythology, namely the story of Zeus, the god and master of all Greek gods, who turned into a white bull with horns dressed in flowers. He stole his mortal love, Europa, away, kidnapping her to Crete, where she later gave birth to the King Minos.

Bulgari
location: Bahnhofstrasse 40.

A NICE PLACE TO REST AWILE...

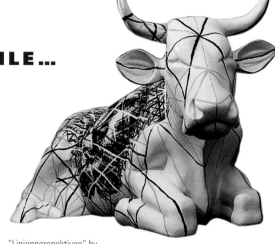

A veritable "Kuh-Sitzbank" (Cow Bench) stands out front of this private bank. One hesitates a bit before sitting down into the seat of this cow, but it is surprisingly comfortable.

There are also the "Menschenkuh" (People Cow), "Die Landschaft ohne Kühe" (The Cow-less Landscape), "Finger Print", "Linienperspektiven" (Line Perspectives) and "Hochseekuh" (High-Seas Cow), a half a dozen cows grazing the area of Bahnhofstrasse/St. Peter-Strasse.

"Linienperspectiven" and "Menschenkuh"
location: corner of Bahnhofstrasse/St. Peter-Strasse 10.

"Linienperspektiven" by
DANIEL SCHMID

(1964). His design evolves out of layers of numerous perspective lines which at their crossing points appear like 3-dimensional shapes jumping out toward the viewer. A lot of work goes into the study of the color layers and the resulting effects. These compositions could be anything – a face or a landscape or even a series of buildings.

"Menschenkuh" by
REGULA STÜCHELI

(1963). The main focus for the artist, here, is the confrontation of the human body and that of the cow. The result is a very original composition. The young artist was discovered at a popular annual exhibition in the city. There, her classic still life – china placed on a table – was made present-day by the fact that the mountain of dishes was drying on a dish rack.

"Hochseekuh" (High Seas Cow) by
HANNES BINDER

(1947). Binder has managed bring about the illusion of waves at high sea, nonetheless, placed upon a very much land-based animal. The waves could also be looked at as a symbol for the ups and downs in life. Hannes Binder is well-known for his illustrations. What looks like wood or linoleum cuts, is actually a texture developed through a process of layering colors which are then selectively scratched away.

"Ruhebank" (Resting Bench) by
DAGMAR HEINRICH

(1953). A bank which has its own "Ruhebank" (Resting Bench) is the unique concept of an artist who has searched for artistic expression through various mediums, like radio work and video performances. For her, the above bench is a place to rest, in contrast to the applied design which represents activity.

"Finger Print" by
CHIARA FIORINI

(1956). The cow, "Mei Ming" (in Chinese "no name") certainly wears her identity well. Her "bar code" perfectly expresses our consumer-oriented society. The work of the artist, who is originally from Ticino, has fluctuated for years between the figurative and abstract. In her paintings, reality and fantasy meet to produce a refined pictorial language.

"Landschaft ohne Kühe" (Cow-less Landscape) by
HENDRIKJE KÜHNE

(1962). Since so many cows have roamed into the city this summer, they're naturally not present in the mountainous regions. The artist, who lives in Basle, depicts them as blank spaces in the landscape.

ORIGINAL

TEAM BLUMEN KRÄMER

created this moss-covered cow.

BETTINA SOLINGER

Atelier DEFACTO, was born in 1961 and resides in Zurich. She works on the conceptualization, layout and realization of exhibitions. She is also an artist in her own right, and enjoys making 3D-objects. Besides the Vidal-Cow, the "Tabak-Viktoria-Kuh" (Victoria Tobacco Cow) was also made by her.

DISPLY TEAM SEIDEN GRIEDER

produced this bewitching beauty.

Direct advertising on the cows is prohibited, but you are certainly allowed, without any hesitation, to make it clear out of which stable they come. In front of Modehaus G., for example, an elegantly dressed beauty gazes out from under a fancy hair-do that's the spitting image of a saddle, while the cow in front of a flower shop is completely covered in moss, out of which little white islands of daisies are growing. And on the other side of the Bahnhofstrasse, an oriental cow in pointed shoes grazes in front of a carpet shop, tassels hanging from the ends of yellow cords wrapped around her waist; and concealed under the red saddlecloth is a curved oriental sword (scimitar).

These original and highly imaginative creations are just three of a whole herd of over 800 street-cows.

left
Blumen Krämer, location: Bahnhofstrasse 38.

p. 87, left:
Vidal AG, location: Bahnhofstrasse 31.

p. 87, right:
Grieder Les Boutiques, location: Bahnhofstrasse 30.

CHIVALRY AMONG COWS

MARLISE GRÄSSLE

graphic designer born in 1948, lives in Gossau ZH. During a 3-year stay in Tenerife, Spain, she worked intensively with glass, and eventually opened her own atelier in 1998 for glass art, decoration, and advertising in Wetzikon.

"Let it be heard throughout time..." (the beginning of a song celebrating a battle fought in the early times of Switzerland). Ever since the days of the quarrelsome mayor and judge, Hans Waldmann, the Zurich Armory has been a sight worth seeing, in which out of town guests of honor, in response to their requests, were shown not only the Zurich Weapons Arsenal but also the Wilhelm Tell's (pretend, of course) crossbow. Today, this medieval structure is put to good use housing one of Zurich's most popular restaurants, the stylish "Zeughauskeller". In line with the old notions of romantic chivalry, chivalrous cows have been selected to beckon passersby, dressed in attire of silver armor covered in precious stones, their hipbones and horns adorned in gold.

Restaurant Zeughauskeller,
location: Bahnhofstrasse 28a, near Paradeplatz.

FABERGÉ SPLENDOR

ALEX ZWAHLEN

Zurich, managed to recreate the Fabergé egg in the form of of a cow. See also pp. 13, 80 and 156.

Antique Collector, location: Banhofstrasse 27.

It recalls the last czar's Easter egg, that splendid cow currently gracing the entrance to the specialty shop, "Antique Collector" on Bahnhofstrasse 27. An especially exquisite sight to see this summer, a conversion of the world-admired Fabergé egg onto the rustic dimensions of a cow's contours. The original art work, which was created in the workshop of the jewelry designer Fabergé and produced by Mikhail Perkhin in Petersburg, just turned 100 this year. In the spring of 1898, on April 5 to be exact, the Czar Nikolaus II gave it to his young wife, Alexandra Feodorovna, as an Easter gift. Today's rendition dons the Romanow coat of arms between its horns, and is covered in countless lilies of the valley, which on the original Easter egg were made out of diamonds and pearls. Tragic fate befell the czar family, when on July 17, 1918 they were executed by communist conspirators behind the Ural in Jekaterinenburg.

STEFAN PLÜSS

lives in Suhr. His artistic interests are in experimental painting, furniture and lighting design. His work was shown at a Christmas exhibition in Kunsthaus Aarau. Plüss has his own atelier in the Fabrik Rüetschi, Suhr. His mouth-watering "Kuh-chen" has met with general approval!

RETO MOROSANI

Bassersdorf, born March 5, 1965. He is trained in silk-screening and welding. In his own atelier, he completes wire-sculptures and objects made out of metal and waste material, from baby strollers to airplanes. Exhibitions: Galleries Büechelerhuus, Glockenhof, Rennweg Gallery, and Heimatwerk Rudolf Brun-Brücke. His "Kuhpferform" is a cow shaped out of copper.

Oh, that scrumptious cake-of-a-cow deliciously situated just outside the very famous pastry shop, Sprüngli. It is quite a feast for the eyes, a real optical delicacy! Just one look at those chocolate-covered legs makes one's mouth water. And oh, how that cow-licious icing makes one want to grab the fork and dig in.

Over 140 years ago, Sprungli was the first to venture into the unclaimed territory of what today is the very famous Paradeplatz. In 1859, in hopes that the new train station would be built directly across the street on the lawn of the Kaserne, this first of Zurich businesses moved from the Marktgasse into the first building on the Fröschengraben (which literally translated means "frogs' trench" and at one time constituted a border around old Zurich). Unfortunately, though, the government had other plans. They informed the public that the new train station would be built directly in the same spot as the original station, (which was situated quite some distance from the Paradeplatz), and instead, they would link it to Paradeplatz by creating what today is the world famous shopping street, the Bahnhofstrasse (Train Station Street). From 1873–76, the Kreditanstalt was built on the Kaserne grounds by Jakob Friedrich Wanner, who also built the Main Train Station from 1865–71.

Confiserie Sprüngli, location: corner of Bahnhofstrasse/Paradeplatz.

NORLANDO POBRE "LANDO"

was born on January 31, 1946 in Alcala, in the Philippines, and has been a Swiss citizen since 1994. In Manila, he learned how to do lithography and photography in a publishing company, after which he went on to study painting and architecture at St. Louis University in Bagio City. He worked in Austria as a painter and restaurater of churches, and in Zurich as a designer of posters. Since 1990, Lando has focused completely on silk painting, creating exclusive hand-painted silk ties and foulards, tops, etc. He is the winner of numerous art prizes and his work has been exhibited in over 200 exhibitions at home and abroad. From the concept of Jürg Bächtold, he has painted, in very fine detail, 26 cows dressed in traditional costume.

The biggest cantonal variety can be found on Paradeplatz where traditional farmer costumes out of every Swiss canton – a total of 26 variations in color, cut and ornamentation – are as becoming on the cows as a sharp business suit or a risqué topless bathing suit.

EBSQU

E. & B. Seeberger-Quin, Zürich, were responsible for concept and realization.

The shops around the Paradeplatz have taken a total of 26 cows and dressed them in traditional costume:

Confiserie Sprüngli AG
CREDIT SUISSE
CREDIT SUISSE PRIVATE BANKING
O. J. Gassmann AG
Daniel B. Hartmann
La Serlas Zürich
Marsano AG
Orell Füssli Hof AG
Savoy Baur en Ville
UBS
A. Türler

THE APPENZELLER COUNTRY

JÜRG BÄCHTOLD

designed the "Trachtenmädchen" (girls in traditional dress), and also the "Karussell Kühe" (Carousel Cows), which symbolize Zurich's world-famous branches: banks, chocolate shops, flowers shops, hotels, fashion, and jewelry. See pp. 10 and 146 for artist's portrait.

The area abounding most in cows in Eastern Switzerland would certainly have to be the hilly Appenzeller country, one of the most impressive examples of the farming industry. Some towns are populated by more cows than kids. The local Alpine pastoral art has become famous through its detailed depiction of what they call the "Alpaufzug", a seasonal ritual procession of bringing the herd of cows up to the mountain meadows. During this procession, the colorful, festive national costumes of the cow herders are most prominently on display.

Our artist has chosen to display the cows in this traditional dress: richly embroidered vests in glowing red and pants in festive yellow.

But the other ladies look resplendent, too, in their fine linen, in shimmering silk, in magnificent embroidery, crochet and lace, in silver jewelry and buckled shoes.

Appenzell

Waadt

Nidwalden

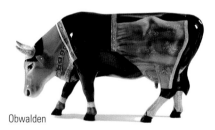
Obwalden

Tessin

Solothurn

Thurgau

Zürich

Fribourg

Genf

Graubünden

Schaffhausen

Luzern

Basel Stadt

COW CAROUSEL

EBSQU

E. und B. Seeberger-Quin, Zürich, are responsible for the conceptualization and realization of the carousel.

Up until 150 years ago, Paradeplatz was called the "Säumärt" (Pig Market), and then later the somewhat improved, "Neumärt" (New Market). It was used as the pig, goat and cattle market. Eventually, though, the city felt compelled to change its name once again, due to the fact that a "Neumarkt" and a "Rindermarkt" had already existed for centuries just on the other side of the city. They decided on the name, "Paradeplatz", from the already existing plaza in Berlin.

In 1882, the "Rösslitram" (a tram pulled by a horse) arrived at the plaza. Currently, three colorful cows are circling merrily around the carousel located on top of the cafe. They are the counterpart to the cow mobile in the main train station.

The carousel is a joint project of Confiserie Sprüngli AG, CREDIT SUISSE, CREDIT SUISSE PRIVATE BANKING, O. J. Gassman AG, Daniel B. Hartmann, La Serlas Zürich, Marsano AG, Orell Füssli Hof AG, Peterhof AG, Savoy Baur en Ville, UBS, A. Türler.

JUST MARRIED

CHARLY BÜHLER

caricaturist, resident of Wila, painted the "Wedding cow" with fertility symbols.

What all can you do with two plastic cows and a lot of white space to fill? Eiermann, a firm which delivers eggs to private households in Zurich, has come up with just one of the many possible answers. Their cow now currently stands outside the entrance to the town hall where, day in and day out, newlyweds make their way to and from the registry office to make things official. A one Mr. Rooster and a lovely Ms. Hen, who themselves have just tied the knot, dash across the cow's belly into honeymoon bliss.

"Eiermaa", location: cloister of the Fraumünster Church, in front of City Hall.

PEGASUS

ARLETTE RICHNER

lives in Baden in the Aargau canton. She is a handcrafts teacher. She organized the international "Figuren-Theaterfestival" (Figure Theater festival) and designed the display windows for Optiker Götte and Zwicker. She created the winged-cows for both firms, with the intention that these heavy animals would appear light enough that they might fly up off into the clouds. It was in the artist's atelier, paradoxically in a vacant used slaughter house, that these cows evolved into the current "Pegasus".

SVEN HARTMANN

designed several cows, this one here being Böhny AG's "Handschuh Kuh" (Glove Cow). Artist's portrait, see p.126.

THE DISPLAY TEAM

of Modehauses Gassmann spread a bit of Parisian and Roman fashion through the city.

One could name the red-winged cows now gracing the entrance from the Münsterhof to Poststrasse in honor of the legendary Greek poet-horse Pegasus. This triplet of cows has found itself a home right where the arcades of the former Posthof have best been preserved.

The Posthof was originally built to house Eastern Swiss Stagecoach Central, and was built to be the most beautiful construction in Switzerland. In 1876, it was indefinitely turned into the Centralhof Department Store, and eventually became a housing block. Most notable is the interior courtyard with arcades, where during the time of the old stagecoaches, the stables were situated, and where for over one hundred years, water has poured out of a tall cast-iron fountain.

Optiker Zwicker, location: Poststrasse 1.

Modehaus Gassmann AG
location: Poststrasse 7.

Böhny AG
location: Poststrasse 5.

THE LATEST IN STORE-FRONT MANNEQUINS

RUTH AND MAX REISER

reside in Zurich. Their work consists mainly of paintings and outdoor sculptures formed out of plastic. It can be seen in the permanent exhibition in Mallorca and in various exhibitions in Germany and Switzerland.

Goldsmith elegance and "fantasy-rich» creations dress the Saint-Phil cows.

According to University of Zurich's Professor Dr. Alfred Hauser, cows used to be much smaller in stature than they are today. Actually, cattle in the 17th century were poorly nourished and produced very little milk, if any at all. This caused a constant shortage of milk in winter, especially in what were typically large families. Back then, milk was the most important source of animal protein. Since there were never more than three cows on the most sophisticated of farms, this resulted in great seasonal differences in the supply and price of milk. For this reason, up into the early 19th century, cheese was only produced in summer months. And it was only first in the late 20th century that tight winter months could be more or less stabilized by using dry feeds like hay.

But things certainly look different today, as is quite clear in the roughly 800 art-cows currently adorning and enlivening Zurich, for they are model figures in size, beauty and overall constitution – such as no farmer has ever seen or bred until now!

Saint-Phil, location: Bahnhofstrasse 26.

right, Saint-Phil, location: Bahnhofstrasse 14.

SKY-BLUE

RODOLPHE RINN

Basle, has subtly designed the Tiffany cow with class.

Bahnhofstrasse 14, address to the world famous, "Tiffany and Company, New York" has captured the world with their glassware, jewelry, and watches of exceptional taste. You can't find a prouder cow than the one now gracing its store front, dressed up in only the best of digs: this art-cow is sitting pretty in Tiffany sky-blue.

Tiffany & Co.
location: Bahnhofstrasse 14.

A FLOCK OF SEAGULLS

PAUL LEBER

is one of the most versatile contemporary Swiss artists. His work ranges from oil paintings, drawings, gouache, lithographs, and etchings to posters, brochures, packaging and illustrations. He was born on May 10, 1928 in Zurich, and currently has a design atelier in the city. Until 1992, he taught at the Kunstgewerbeschule in Zurich, and for many years was responsible for the artistic direction of Zurich's Artists Masked Balls. His work can be found in many public and private collections at home and abroad. (picture: Paul Leber and his son.)

Kuh Coop, see pg. 60.

vibrantly decorate the pair of cows belonging to the well-known Weinberg Fashions on upper Bahnhofstrasse. Years ago, this firm with an artistic flair for stylish women's and men's clothing, chose the seagull as its logo.

Weinberg-Mode, location: Bahnhofstrasse 13.

PARISIAN STYLE

LANOÉ JOÉLLE

Zurich, born 1964, works as a self-employed painter and illustrator in Zurich. Her work has been exhibited in single exhibitions in various galleries in the city. "Rägi" is her cow's name.

WALTER KNAPP

lives in Stäfa, worked for a long period for Jelmoli as Director of the Display Department. Already for the big lion festival ten years ago, his was a great contribution. He is actually the one who came up with the idea for this summer's Cow Parade, which in hindsight, involved a lot of hard work and brought with it many problems, although his previous experience and contacts made while working on the project with the lions were a blessing.

He, himself, helped to fill the pastures with quite a few cows: for Christ, for Jelmoli, and also for the City Association, itself. On the right page are his "Brillen-Tiere" (Eye-Glass Animals).

Alfred Day AG
location: Bahnhofstrasse 12.

right page, KOCH OPTIK AG
location: Bahnhofstrasse 11.

Bahnhofstrasse 12, along with some of its neighboring buildings, has to this day maintained the look of an historical Parisian boulevard. The fact that Modehaus Day has also upheld its great sense of style and tradition is reflected in its colorful cow which reflect the fresh colors of the rain forest.

SPONSORING WITH HEART

JOHANN A. SONDEREGGER

born 1943, lives in Marthalen. Following an apprenticeship in graphic design in Wintherthur and an education on the Kunstgewerbeschule, he worked in an atelier in Zurich for 9 years. Since 1973, he has been working in his own atelier where he specializes in cartoon illustration, book illustration and designing brochures. He also makes architectural perspectives, murals and designs objects.

He has designed five "theater cows" for the Zürcher Kantonalbank: theatrical figures and scenes are depicted through pictograms, using strong black lines, whose strokes work with the contours of the cows' bodies. The results are spectacular and full of life.

More often than not, sponsoring is just a cover for nothing more than you give me what I want and I'll give you something in return. But the Zürcher Kan-

Scenes from a theater in Kanton Zurich
Zürcher Kantonalbank, location: Bahnhofstrasse 9.

tonalbank, does things differently. In fact, they've taken this summer's event as an opportunity to bring attention to needy theaters in the canton of Zurich.

CLASSICAL

FRÉDÉRIQUE WINTER (CHOPIN)

was born in Kassel, Germany in 1957. She studied graphic design in Munich and has worked as an artist since 1982, having exhibited alone and in groups in Switzerland, Germany and Austria. She lives and works in Zurich as well as in the canton Ticino. Since 1987, she has created murals and trompes l'oeil. The themes of her work, for example the boundlessness of creation, reflect the attempt to express a person's inner beauty.

Winter decorated the cow for the Nationalbank with motifs out of Greek antiquity, which provides it with a timeless elegance.

Schweizerische Nationalbank
location: corner of
Börsenstrasse/Bahnhofstrasse.

At one time, the banks of Lake Zurich extended all the way out to the lot of what is today's Nationalbank, and was only first filled in at the start of the 19th century. It was there that in 1877 the Börsenstrasse was developed and later in 1922 the Nationalbank. Built in 1922, the bank is known as the most beautiful building of the period between World War I and II.

MONIKA ZIMMERMAN

born on April 19, 1968, was educated as a textile designer. Her
preferred art form, however, is
comic illustration. In that field, she
has participated in many competitions and received prizes. She uses
many different media to produce
both her comics and illustrations.
She lives in Zurich and is the
mother of a 3-month old baby. The
artist has depicted the excellent
service at Hotel Baur au Lac with
a magical touch.

Hotel Baur au Lac
location: Garden on the corner of Talstrasse / Börsenstrasse.

BURKLIPLATZ

ERICH GRUBER

works as a graphic designer, illustrator, painter and cartoonist. Since 1971, he has been self-employed, working from his own atelier. His "Tiger-Kühe", is a great advertisement for the Zurich Zoo's wildlife preservation campaign.

BEAT ANDREAS BRUNNER

Sculptura, St. Gallen, born 1961. Following an apprenticeship in a bakery, he attended the Kunstgewerbeschule. In the last ten years, Sculptura has focused mainly on building snow sculptures. Significant projects include Schneedorf Arosa (1995) and the new town sculpture in Braunwald (skiing resort). The group designed a series of five cows for: GAST-Gemeinschaft Autofreier Schweizer Tourismusorte, Braunwald Rails (p. 13), Märchenhotel Braunwald, Mürren Tourismus and the Sport Hotel Stoos.

The lovely, and above all, bright and sunny, Bürkliplatz is one of the nicest spots in Zurich. It was built by city engineer, Arnold Bürkli (1853–1854). Bürkli also built the Quaibrücke and the Bahnhofstrasse, which finally brought a direct connection between railway and shipping. In 1908, Bürkliplatz was given the city engineer's name, and received a memorial plaque in his honor.

Zurich Zoo, location: Bürkliplatz

right page, Gast Mürren Tourismus, location: Bürkliplatz.

A COLORFUL TRANSFORMATION

THE KUONI DISPLAY TEAM

have let their cows graze along the Bellevue pastures. Their cows spark the impulse to travel. Other cows by Kuoni can be seen on pp. 27 and 156.

CLAUDIA LORETZ

Oberdorf, is a housewife and in her spare time, an artist. Her passion for mosaics spilled over onto her richly ornate cow.

GERHARD MÜLLER

Dietikon, designed a whole cow herd – one for Micro-Electric Hörservice (p. 27), his own, as well as four for Welti Furrer AG, (p. 117).

PETER RECK

Agno, decorated the sweet temptress "Edelweiss" for Alprose.

Certainly Zurich's transformation into a merry little Alpine meadow is not necessarily art in the true sense of the word. All the more spontaneous and stronger the general enthusiasm has been, though. Already on the first day, these colorful cows and the rarely seen gorgeous weather drew in tens of thousands of admiring crowds to the downtown. "Zurich is a really beautiful and, moreover, imaginative city!" This enthusiasm was everywhere to be heard, from the train station to Burkliplatz and Bellevue, where the golden holy cows where especially admired. Up to its final days in the fall, the City Association, which planned, organized and realized this whole event, is hoping for one million additional city visitors to come see the spectacle.

right page
Welti Furrer AG, right chocolate Alprose SA, location: Bellevue.

Kuoni Reisen AG, location: Bellevue.

Claudia Loretz, location: near Bellevue.

A HEAVY LOAD

MAGDA BLAU

Merlischachen, turned a cow into a bike racer. See also p.19.

ROSEMARIE LANG

lives in Geroldswil. She devotes her time to "Bauernmalerei", also teaching the craft in her own school. The cow located on the pier, painted in city and folklore imagery with a richly decorated cow bell, depicts the relationship between city and country.

GERHARD MÜLLER

Dietikon. The "Schwergewicht" (Heavyweight) for Welti Furrer is his work. From the same artist, see pp. 27, 35 and 115.

HEINZ BLUM

painted the "Baslerin" (The Woman from Basle). See also pp. 30/31, 138 and 156.

Velo-Import
Christof A. Schmid, Horgen
location: Limmatquai/Marktgasse.

Including the pedestals on which they stand, each cow weighs in at 200 kilos (approx. 500lbs.) – that's no light matter! But looking at them, they appear so light and cheerful, just like the crowds of admirers that surround them each day. Happiness is in the air, everywhere, even the cows seem to be singing with joy. They appear to be looking out on this world of ours, full of spirit as they calmly stand there, their trusting eyes unswerving, as little squirts hop on top of them to play cowboy, or Japanese tourists take snapshots for the folks back home.

right page, Welti Furrer AG, location: Limmatquai.

right, Pier 7, location: Limmatquai, Pier 7.
Here's a place to quench your thirst along your cow stroll.
Basler Versicherungen, location: Limmatquai.

THE BEST IN LEATHER

RAHEL ARNOLD

lives in Hausen am Albis.

ERWIN EGGIMANN

"Eggi" lives in Horgen. He is the creator of the mural of the city Alpine pasture.

JAN LEISER

Zurich, created in addition to the "Läder-Chue" (Leather Cows), two cows for Hotel Sofitel Zürich. See p. 148.

AUGUST WINIGER
BRIGITT BURKHARD

live in Hausen am Albis. This stylish cow is the collaborative work of the Winigers. Brigitt Winiger-Burkhard developed the design and color-concept, and her husband, Gusti, carried it out. He also did another cow for Eurochic.

Büro Fürrer AG
location: Münsterhof 13.

Leder-Locher, located for over 150 years at the Münsterhof, specializes in luggage, handbags and suitcases. Its oldest display items, of original production, are older than the Railways. Its current hand-crafted specialties include leather straps, belts, handbags, and suitcases all made from genuine leather.

Leder Locher AG, cow on the left from Jan Leiser; cow in the middle from Rahel Arnold, Eurochic Leder AG, Mettmenstetten; cow on the right from August Winiger, Brigitte Burkhard, location: Münsterhof 18. View of the Zurich Alps, Büro Fürrer AG, designed by Erwin Eggimann, location: Münsterhof 13.

NOBLE

HEIDI MISEREZ

born in Schwarzwald, has lived in Stallikon since 1953. She originally studied to be a designer/stylist. A 12-year journey over four different continents and the ensuing interaction with other cultures eventually brought her to a new start in her life. She attended a series of courses at well-known schools for photography, painting and design. Her work, which can be seen in many Swiss galleries, expresses the enigmatic, making it visible and perceptible. Her "Meister-Kuh" (Master Cow) is designed in the art of Tiffany glass.

The Münsterhof, at the foot of the in 874 christened Fraumünster, once served as a courtyard to this noble women's cloister. It was the only possible place in the city, as all other larger clearings in the densely developed town lay outside of the medieval city wall. Today, the Münsterhof is Zurich's most prestigious plaza, housing two large guild houses and various prominent boutiques and shops.

Meister Silber AG, location: Zunfthaus Meisen, Münsterhof 20.

DADDY LONGLEGS

MICHAEL HEUSI

was born in Zurich in 1970. He studied interior architecture and product design at the Höhere Schule für Gestaltung. The "Storchengasse" concept is his, which he also developed and realized. With the exception of the "Tabakuh", he designed all of the cows.

ATELIER AROMA

Lukas Meier was put in charge of carrying out the Storchengasse cows. The finished designs resulted from a close collaboration with Michael Heusi, "Ferrari"; with Carmen d'Apollonia, "Passant" and "Badende"; with Monika Baàn, the "Schachspielerin" and the "Störchinnen"; with Werner Baumgartner, the "Kuhmäleon"; with Blimbo, "Aston Martin"; the "Königin" with Sereina Borner.

The Association of Storchengasse and Strehlgasse designed these eleven cows under one common theme – each cow symbolizes the area in which it is exhibited. The "Storchenkühe" (Stork Cows) walks on stilts through the Storchengasse. "Passant" (Passer-by) sticks its curious head through a storefront window. One almost trips over the "Kuhmäleon" (Cowmeleon) – which blends in with the cobblestone pavement. "Tabakuh" (Tobacco Cow) and the "Schachspielerin" (Chess Player) are enjoying themselves on the Weinplatz, looking on in amazement at the daring "Badende" (Swimmer) getting ready to take a dip into Zurich's cool waters. And high above them all, rules the noble "Königskuh" (Royal Cow).

"Ferrari-Kuh" and "Kuhmobil", location: no parking zone in front of the entrance to Storchengasse / corner of Münsterhof.

"Passant" (Passerby), location: Löw, Storchengasse.

"Storchenkühe" (Stork Cows), location: Storchengasse.

DELICACIES FROM THE SOUTH

The picturesque Weinplatz, which from 1630 to 1674 was the location for a public market selling domestic wines, was very likely already in the Roman times (15 BC – 401 AD) the trade center for southern wines, spices, olive oil and other such delicacies, as it was here that the antique harbor, thermal baths and the Limmatbrücke were located. Standing as proud reminders of this rich past are the two oldest buildings remaining on this plaza, the early 15th century Hotels Rote Schwert, whose entrance to this day is framed by a sword, and, directly opposite, the Storchen, the most famous building in the old town. The former municipal Kornhaus once stood in front of these buildings, along the water, where today a cow stands perched at the edge of a springboard overlooking the Limmat, demure in her bathing suit, and yet a bit hesitant as she stands ready to jump. Is the water too cold?

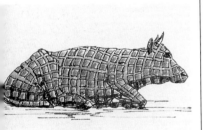

Sketch of the "Kuhmäleon" (Cow-meleon), Spitzbarth Zürich location: Weinplatz 7.

"Königskuh" (Royal Cow), Pastorini AG, location: Weinplatz.

"Schachspielerin" (Chess Player), location: Weinplatz.

Toni Lopardo, "Die Badende", location: Hotel Storchen, Weinplatz.

SACRIFICIAL ANIMALS

URSULA DÖRIG

resident of Uster, designer for Marinello, creator of the fruit and vegetable cows.

GYMNASIUM RÄMIBÜHL

Ranging from 16 to 19 years old, the drawing class of Gymnasium Rämibühl have painted the cow for the Sihltal Zurich Uetliberg Bahn.

Cattle rituals have existed for thousands of years, even in Zurich. This summer's "Cow Parade" unknowingly ties the knot on a virtually prehistoric ritual. Back in earlier times, year after year, most often in the springtime, hedonistic goddesses were offered up sacrifices. Most of these sacrifices were performed using livestock. Far into the times of Christianity, Zurich's festively crowned sacrificial animals were ritualistically led in a festive procession to the slaughter house.

Documentation:
In a lithograph dated 1855, six butchers, to the applause of onlookers, are depicted leading six crowned Easter oxen over the Rathausbrücke to the slaughter house. (Graphic collection Central Library Zurich)

SZU, Sihltal Zürich Uetliberg Bahn, location: Rathausbrücke (Gemüsebrücke).

Marinello, location: Rathausbrücke
(Gemüsebrücke)

HAPPY CITY-COWS

SVEN HARTMANN

The artist living on the Schipfe-strasse in Zurich has mixed roots: on April 8, 1943, he was born in Bellinzona to a Dutch mother and a Swiss father. It was there, in the Italian surroundings, that his love for art, good wine and fine kitchen were also born. After finishing his studies in display design, he turned more to drawing. He was first a student, and then later, a professor at the Kunstgewerbeschule in Zurich and in Basle. Later, he turned to making films, as well as creating puppets and larger-than-life figures out of cardboard. He then created a series of stories about a cat named Jacob, a character that has become eternalized through hundreds of such stories. Sven Hartmann's greatest passions are drawing and painting from still life. He created the fantasy-rich designs for Blumen Schipfe, Böhny Handschuhe, Tabaklädeli Wagner-Gerbig with the master touch of a talented artist.

was the headline for a series of editorial letters in the Tagesanzeiger. The following is an excerpt from one of the more endearing letters:

"A daisy would not want to be a rose, and both are equally beautiful. On Sunday, I went to see the cows in Zurich. And I would do it again and again and again. I do not share the opinion of the "experts" who referred to all of this as a "folklore-boom". "Does this sound a bit arrogant? I'm sure I must just be imagining things, because the Zurich cows are so lovely, both the plastic and the real ones, which I don't like any less. An wonderful source of pleasure and fun has been created out of a simple piece of plastic. From behind those long eyelashes they look out at you, as they blink coquettishly or study their visitors with curious eyes. Crowned in flowers, spotted and striped, adorned with butterflies dancing across their bellies, alight with alpineglow and golden wings, which make it seem as if at any moment they will fly off into the sky. The children stare in amazement, and even many of the adults find themselves feeling like a kid, again.
I would like to extend my thanks to all artists for their creativity, humor and imagination. I think I'll go pet those cows, tell them how funny there are and let them know they make my heart sing."

Blumen Schipfe AG. location: Schipfe 25.

DREAMY...

**THOMAS GÜNTER
SYLVIA HAUBER
CLAIRE SCHMID**

Zurich, collaborated in creating the "Glückskuh" (Lucky Cow).

SVEN HARTMANN

Zurich, painted the playful penguin. See also pp. 85 and 126.

JUTYA HUNDT

from Zurich, decorated the "Kinder-mode-Kuh" (Children's Fashion Cow), with a delicate garland and toys.

Täuber AG, location: Schipfe 24/26.

A. Günter. location: Schipfe 43.

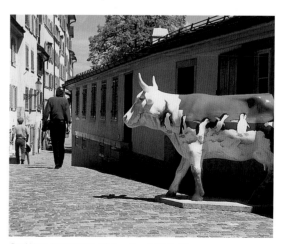

Dani Vock Antiquitäten AG, location: Schipfe 10.

"LIÔBA, LIÔBA..."

RUTH HELLER

Etcher, wife, mother, owner of dogs, cats and fish, fashion boutique owner, salesperson, painter with her own atelier and owner of a card manufacturing store, lives in Au/SG. This varied lady – she is left-handed – also designed a water bottle for bikes, exclusively for Heimatwerke der Schweiz. The original "Switzerland-Bottle" is colorfully decorated using a silk-screen technique. Her colorful cards, either hand-painted or repro-duced in small series, are funny, warm, and sometimes a bit cheeky. She paints impressionistic figures and animals, but also creates abstract color compositions, often times in 3-dimensional collages. She likes to use a mixture made up of fine sand and linseed oil, colored by pigments.

The "Heimatwerk-Kuh" is dedicated to children.

All over, customs are undergoing change. This inclu-des local dialects. Who would still know, today, that far into this present century, the cow, was once affectionately referred to as a "Loobe" or "Loobeli". The origins of this traditional expression is unclear, but it is certain that it was used over quite an expan-sive distance, reaching over the boundaries of lan-guage. For example, up in the high reaches of the French-speaking region, La Gruyère, a reservoir of traditional culture, not only do they breed cattle and produce a world-famous cheese, but to the pride of the "Armailli", as the dairymen are referred to, they are known to sing, over and over with great enthu-siasm, a melodic Alpine "cow rhyme" called "Liôba". At sunset, they go up into the mountains and sing this song in honor of the cows.

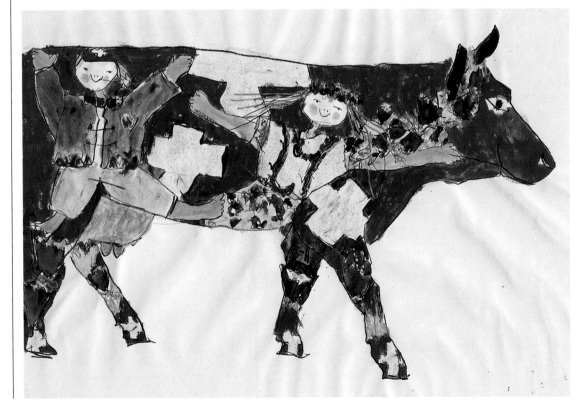

Schweizer Heimatwerk
location: Rudolf-Brun-Brücke.

JÜRG HILDEBRAND

from Creative Atelier, created the "Japanese Lady".

PIETRO MARTINI

Unterengstringen, stylized the "Gelockte" (Curly)

ELSO SCHIAVO

Baar, painted the "Apothekerin" (The Pharmacist) coram publico, on site. He also used his creative hands to design the cow for the Schweizer Tierschutz, and also Peter Keck AG. Artist portrait, see p. 48.

right page, from the left, Hotel Ascot, L'arco blu GmbH, Hairstyling, Enge Apotheke, location: Tessinerplatz 3, 5, 7.

7000 years of cows in Zurich? In the dry winter of 1853/54, the first remains of a pile dwelling village were discovered along the banks of Obermeilen on Lake Zurich. All of Europe looked on in fascination. These native inhabitants originally settled as lakeside dwellers, cultivating land and raising small cow herds. The animals were mainly used as meat stock; how much milk they actually produced is uncertain. Over time, these pile dwellers' knowledge and way of life spread out from Zurich across the whole of Europe. Among the artifacts found were beautifully-formed pottery, some early fabrics, and also tools and utensils of all kinds, many of which were made out of cattle bones.

The most significant inheritance the pile dwellers passed on was cattle herding, for which Zurich, through this summer's festivities, give thanks, as it was on the little port, a former island near the Bellevue, just above Quaibrucke, that one of the most notable pile dwellings once existed.

In addition, the Swiss Landesmuseum, located behind the train station, which opened its doors on January 15, 1898 and this summer celebrates its 100 year anniversary, was originally founded from the studies made on researchers in pile dwelling villages.

DEPICTING THE COW

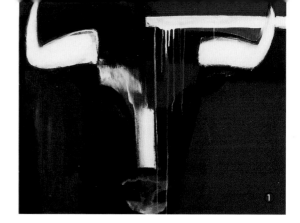

GARDA ALEXANDER

was born in Landau an der Isar in 1961. Following gymnasium, she studied in Columbia, attended the drawing school, "Zeiler" in Munich, Schule für Gestaltung in Zurich, and the School of Fine Arts in Bebegeny, Hungary. She has participated in various international projects.

IRÈNE CURIGER

was born in Zurich. She attended the Kunstgewerbeschule Zürich. She also studied in Salzburg and Maissau in the summer months, and took a student trip to Asia, Eygpt, Afrika and the U.S. She won 1st prize in an exhibition in Helsinki, and won a prize in Wintherthur's, "Kunst in der Stadt".

ANITA GENTINETTA

Mettmenstetten, born in 1938, paints using a mixed technique of gouache and oil.

ANNA REGULA HARTMANN

ANNA, born in 1941, has studied the human both on the outside (in art) and on the inside (in medicine). She lives and works in Basle as a painter for exhibitions, books and newspapers.

GALERIE COMMERCIO
Mühlbachstrasse 2 (Stadelhofen).

is the name of the group exhibition, cow as theme, currently showing in Galerie Commercio, which incidentally celebrates its 25th anniversary this year. A total of 23 artists from Winterthur to Neuenburg, from Basle to Lugano, from Leipzig to Milano, have dealt with the theme of this prehistoric animal through paintings, illustrations, drawings, woodcuts, sculptures and tapestry. A few haven't taken the theme too seriously, which is o.k. by the owner of the gallery, Pia Peter. All are of high quality and could easily soon become collector's items. After all, it isn't everyday that a cow is painted, drawn or carved by such well-known artists like Irène Curiger, Christiane Dubois, Caspar Frei, Susanne Keller, Ernst Ludwig Kirchner, Hans Krüsi, Paul Leber, Ulf Puder or Christophe Vorlet.

Garda Alexander ①
untitled
80 x 92 cm, acrylic on canvas

Irène Curiger ②
"Maskerade", 1998
45 x 60 cm, mixed technique on cardboard.

Anita Gentinetta ③
untitled
80 x 100 cm, mixed technique

Anna Hartmann ④
untitled

Mietervereinigung Bahnhof Stadelhofen, location: Bahnhof Stadelhofen.

AT STADELHOFER PLATZ

PAUL BERCHTOLD

born 1976, lives in Adliswil. He is a trainee at the Basler Versicherungen. In his free time, he is a "paint brusher". He designed both of his cows using this technique. One stands in front of Bahnhof Stadelhofen, the other in front of Bahnhof Wiedikon.

NICOLA CONDOLEO

from Opfikon, created the "Stahl-Kuh" (Steel Cow). See p. 133 (left).

RETO HUBER

lives in Uetikon. «Kuh-Kuh» (Cow-Cow) is the name of his design. See p. 133 (right).

BARBARA ZOLLINGER

and her team designed the "Silberne" (Silver One) in front of the restaurant "Zum Olivenbaum".

Basler Versicherung
location: Stadelhofer Platz.

right page, ZFV Unternehmungen
location: Stadelhoferstrasse 10.

On the filled-in ground of the once existing entrenchment of the Stadelhofer suburb, the "Haus zum Olivenbaum" was built in 1838, in place of the Stadelhoferpforte from 1678. In the later part of the Biedermeier, the Stadelhofer Platz was developed, trees planted and a cast-iron fountain erected. The train station was built in 1893/94 as the railway line to the right bank of the lake.

150 YEARS AGO

MARIE-CHRISTINE BÜCHI-JABIOLLE

born in 1957, lives today in Utikon. She received her doctorate in Philosophy I, spanish (this study encompasses languages, art and philosophy). Her artistic career began in 1990. Since 1993, she has exhibited in Basle, Germany, and France.

Her cows appear full of life and color.

URSULA RUTISHAUSER

Feldmeilen, born 1965. She studied to be a display designer and has had experience working on the construction of fairs. She is currently attending the Scuola di Sculptura in Maggiatal.

W. Kandinsky's "Le Ciel" was the inspiration for her "Himmelskuh" (Heaven's Cow).

PETER WISKEMANN

Männedorf. Along with the children from the Malschule Fred Zemp, Männerdorf, he created the fantastic images on this cow.

Rechte Seite: Mietervereinigung Stadelhofer Passage
location: Stadelhofer Passage.

Kramer Gastronomie
location: Dufourstrasse 4.

A brief look at the Zurich cattle business 150 years ago: "Cattle breeding, an inseparable component of farming, has in recent times been given considerable attention in some regions; still, farmers could do a lot more for it. Cattle breeding is in a blossoming state in the districts of Affoltern and Horgen, and some areas of the districts Zurich, Meilen and Regensberg, and much less in remaining districts. But no where is it completely neglected. In the surrounding regions of Zurich, many cattle owners place their pride in raising beautiful, healthy cows."

A MUSICAL PLAZA

CHRISTOPH BERNET

born in 1962 in St. Gallen, has lived in Zurich since 1966. He started out apprenticing as a painter, and built his way up to being foreman. From 1989, he specialized in decorative painting. From 1990, he began to focus his work on the restaurant and hotel branches. Since 1995, he has been working out of his own atelier. His baroque "Florhof-Dame" is romantically adorned.

HEINZ BLUM

Zurich, has brought a total of 17 cows to this pasture, see pp. 30/31 and 116 and 156. The curtains have opened and his stars have come out on stage.

ANJA LAHUSEN

Zurich, is currently studying on the Schule für Gestaltung. She has tuned the keys to perfection on her musical cows.

Hotel Du Théâtre
location: Seilergraben 69.

Heimplatz, location to the little-known monument to the singer, Ignaz Heim, is also home this summer to the cows of Jecklin, a music store located on Rämistrasse 30–42. The former restaurant, "Pfauen" used to be located here in house no. 30. The whole plaza, officially the Heimplatz, is still refered to as "Pfauen" to this day, location to the former Pfauentheater (today a playhouse). Gottfried Keller used to come to this historical restaurant. And today, Jecklin has picked the perfect setting, an area once devoted to the fine arts, to promote its music shop in the form of musical-looking cows.

Jecklin Musikalienhandlung, location: Rämistrasse 30.

right page, the romantic Hotel Florhof, location: Florhofgasse 4.

THE ALPS COME TO LIFE

IRIS ELSNER

from Bremgarten, KVZ employee, oversaw the whole operation, contributed her own inspiring ideas and lent an eager hand, as well, both during the design and production.

HANS JÖRG VON KÄNEL

the well-known artist lives in Zurzach. His cows are the result of tremendous creativity and range in style and technique.

BENO SCHULTHESS

lives and works in Widen, as well as his second home in Brissago. He is a well-known artist, who has made a name for himself through his sculptures and fountain objects, one of which stands in the Sportzentrum Magglingen. His contribution to the event: "La Vache Fédérale" (The Federal Cow).

The romantic notion of being a cow herder is not just idyll dreaming in Letzipark. And the Alpine hut, Alphorn players and the 13 colorful cows certainly do bring it to life. But what really makes it authentic is the installed cheese-dairy which lures in interested onlookers. It is set-up for making everything from semi-hard to soft cheeses, and each step of the process – from the heating of the milk to the forming of the loaves – is shown and explained. And as at any cheese-dairy, one can taste-test samples of the dairy's creations, which is certainly a great opportunity to become more familiar with the incredibly broad range of cheeses in Switzerland.

Ten fantastic cows have come to be as the result of a competition put on by the employees of Letzipark Shopping Center. The ideas were then carried out in team-work. First prize went to Iris Elsener for her design of the "Esoterik-Kuh" (Esoteric Cow).

Cows 1–13:
Konsum Verein Zürich
location: Letzipark.

① **«Meer-Kuh»**
Idea and Design: Hansjörg von Känel.

② **«La Vache Fédérale»**
Idea and Design: Bruno Schulthess.

③ **«Kuhraffe»**
Idea: Regula von Gunten. Design: Hansjörg von Känel.

④ **«Südsee»**
Idea and Design: Hansjörg von Känel.

⑤ **«Königin der Nacht»**
Idea: Edith Quattrini. Design: Hansjörg von Känel.

⑥ **«Titanic»**
Idea: Regula von Gunten. Design: Display-Team E. Schuler, Schlieren.

⑦ **«Akt-Kuh»**
Idea and Design: Hansjörg von Känel.

⑧ **«Letzipark-Kuh»**
Idea: Iris Elsner. Design: Eva Bohnenblust.

⑨ **«Holzkuh»**
Idea: Detlev Elsner. Design: Hansjörg von Känel.

⑩ **«Esoterik-Kuh»**
Idea and Design: Iris Elsner.

⑪ **«Blumen-Kuh»**
Idea: Monika Bissig. Design: Iris Elsner/Anja Foigt.

⑫ **«Papageien-Kuh»**
Idea: Regula von Gunten. Design: Iris Elsner/Eva Bohnenblust.

⑬ **«Letzi-Fenster»**
Idea and Design: Iris Elsner.

①

141

AT STAUFFACHER

F+F
FARBE UND FORM

Schule für Experimentelle Gestaltung, Zürich. Under the direction of Agnes Wyler, the students worked in teams dressing up their cows in an auto bodyshop on the Badenerstrasse. The cows have been wonderfully designed in a variety of techniques and styles.

The Streets Association of Stauffacher and its members organized the design of eleven cows, asking the school for experimental design, F+F, to paint them. From a whole pile of conceptual sketches, the association selected the nicest ones to be produced.

The theft of one of the cows caused a big stir. It has not showed up to this day.

Rex, Mäntel und Jacken, location: Zweierplatz/Badenerstrasse 60.

Restaurant Emilio (left), Credit Suisse, location: Badenerstrasse 50.

Elektro Göbel AG, Lutherstrasse 6: cow stolen – location?

OLD PATHWAYS – LUSH MEADOWS

SONIA C. CASANOVA

born in Zurich, and lives here today. She originally apprenticed to be a leather goods salesperson, and later a receptionist. This artist's strengths lie in the love for the small and delicate, as well as a strong sense for color. Her artistic interests started with classical porcelain painting, followed by the application of modern color compositions onto the porcelain, as well as on to silk, and eventually onto canvas with acrylic and spatula. Since 1981, she has run her own atelier and taken part in various exhibitions.
Colorful butterflies and shimmering lizards painted spring green make up the decor of her "Waid-Kuh" (Meadow Cow).

JÜRG FURRER

born in 1939, is married and lives in Seon. He is a cartoonist, artist and illustrator. In 1966, he produced his first drawings for the journal, Nebelspalter. Today, he works for various publications among them Tages-Anzeiger, Süddeutsche Zeitung, Playboy, illustrating as well children's books and school books. His work has been exhibited worldwide. His cows for the Grand Hotel are wearing red bows in celebration of the hotel's 100-year anniversary.

Just how closely connected this city once was with the surrounding farmland, particularly cow herding, can still be seen in the names of meadows and streets, some of which have maintained their old luster to this day. Records show that already back in 1277, reference was made to the "Rindermarkt" (Cattle Market). Probably as old, the "Milchbuck", a small alpine meadow situated in the vicinity of the city up on a hill near Oerlikon, was once a lucrative cow pasture. Today, it can be recalled in the street name, "Milchbuckstrasse" which dates back to 1927. Up into the 1800's, some Zurchers kept their milking cows just out back in a shed behind the house. Early in the morning, these animals would be gathered together by a co-operatively employed cow herder, and then led out along the Rennweg and Oberdorfstrasse, and across the city commons in Hard, and then taken up into today's Zurichberg neighborhood. This is how the "Rämistrasse", located in front of the city wall, got the name it carried from 1929– 1865, "Kuhgasse" (Cow Lane). The same such name existed in Hottingen up into Gottfried Keller's times, the later Hofstrasse to the Alp Dreiwiesen. In Hirslanden, the "Kühweg" (Cow Way) wound up into the Zurichberg, and a "Hirtenweg"(Cattle Way) has memorialized the former cow community since its development in 1903. In Selnau, up into the early 19th century, there was a "Chue-Brugg" (Cow Bridge) which was used to lead the cows over the Sihl canal. In Wiedikon, there was a

bull pasture for breeding animals in "Heuried", which was also called the "Gemeindemuni" (bull community). Along two properties of the "Pfingstweidstrasse" (Pentecost Pasture Street), located in today's industry quarters, cattle were once led just after Pentecost when the grass had grown back nicely. The "Waidstrasse" (Pasture Street) is situated in the Wipkinger cattle pasture, where a popular scenic restaurant once stood during the Biedermeier era, and in 1907 the Waid Hospital was built.

Looked at from this point of view, this summer's cow-event is a folkloric memorial in honor of a tradition-rich centuries-old past. It is perhaps too seldom noticed that many features of these old rituals still live on today, remaining contemporary.

Restaurant Neue Waid, location: Waidberg.

right page
view of the lake and city, Dolder Grand Hotel, location : Kurhausstrasse 66.

ALL THE WAY TO ZÜRICH-NORD

JÜRG BÄCHTOLD

Zumikon, turned the cows for the pharmacy into a blooming field, see p. 149. Other cows by the artist can be seen on pp. 10/11, 92, 98 and 152.

Artist porträt, see p. 10.

RUDOLF H. STETTLER

born in 1944, he lives and works today in Bern. Originally a textile engineer, information scientist and sales manager, today he is one of the most successful artists in the Federal capital. His paintings hang in banks, villas and public buildings. His cow, "LISA", designed for Herrenmode Ruchti, already had storms of interested buyers straight from the start.

KURT WINIGER

Zurich, designed the gastronomic cow "Kroni". See p. 70/71.

This urban cow pasture rolls out along Unterstrass and Oberstrass, all the way out to Oerlikon. The lower street, leading from the former Niederdorf gate over the Milchbuck in the direction of Schaffhausen – today, called Stampfenbachstrasse and Schaffhauserstrasse – is the spine of the Unterstrass neighborhood. Oberstrass, which got its name from the in 1893 incorporated linear village situated along the upper street, runs in the direction of Wintherthur.

To the delight of residents, the Trade Association Unterstrass/Oberstrass launched the opening ceremonies with an "Alpaufzug" (Alpine procession) through both neighboring quarters.

left to right
Schaffhauserplatz-Apotheke, location: Schaffhauserplatz/Seminarstrasse. Hotel Restaurant Krone Unterstrass, location: Schaffhauserstrasse 1. Herrenmode Ruchti, location: Beckenhofstrasse 70/72.

SCHOOL FOR COW KEEPERS

JAN LEISER

was born in Zurich in 1965, and lives here, today. Following an apprenticeship in carpentry, he attended the Kunstgewerbeschule Zürich, where he studied interior architecture and product design. He worked on the "Heureka" and "Phänomena" exhibtions. Leiser's paintings are both naturalistic and surrealistic. His paintings have something somewhat mystical about them. He also works in the areas of ceramics and photography.

Alongside of his hotel-cows, he designed the "Läder-Chue" (Leather Cows), p. 118.

The cantonal agricultural school Strickhof, which opened on city grounds in 1852 near the former Milchbuck pasture, is the oldest agricultural school of Switzerland. At that time, the farm encompassed 51.2 acres. The stables contained 56 young Simmentaler and brown milking cows, 42 bovines, and in addition, 400 pigs and 900 chickens. In the mid-1970's, the University of Zurich claimed a part of the lot for additional buildings due to the increasing population of students. On the search for a new suitable location, the agricultural school came upon the Weiler Eschlikon, located in the community Lindau, near the Zurich-Winterthur highway, where the new school was furnished to run as the agricultural educational center from 1974–1976. Comprised of the "Research, Counseling and Education" departments, the new school quickly achieved international importance.

Hotel Sofitel, location: Stampfenbachstrasse 60.

Schaffhauserplatz-Apotheke, location: Schaffhauserplatz/Seminarstrasse.

THE ALPINE FESTIVAL IN OERLIKON

LE BOUCHER CORPAATO

Fribourg, shows another of his large urban cow herd. See also p. 66/67, 70 and 82.

WILLI FREUDIGER

Wetzikon, created the stylish lady in the glasses, see p. 153.

HANS PETER STEINER

from Zurich, presents his black flower-girl. See also pp. 154/155.

Café City, Chäs-Bächler/Fehlmann Früchte und Gemüse, Metzgerei Ziegler, Wanner Optik/Into-Boutique, Vereinigung "Z'Oerlike gits alles", location: Welchogasse.

Zurich-Nord also caught the cow paradefever. The approximate 25 members of the association, "z'Oerlike gits alles" (Oerlikon has everything) have brought fantasy-rich colorful cows out onto the streets of the "Stadt vor der Stadt" (city before the city) and have given the northern part of the city a

Cafeteria City, Chäs-Bächler/Fehlmann Früchte und Gemüse.

colorful flair. With the "Alpaufzug" (Alpine procession), the retailers on the Welchogasse applauded the cow herd with the jingle of their alphorn bells and the sounds of gay folk music.

Köbi Möri Beschriftungen, (Sunflowers), Metzgerei Ziegler.

JÜRG BÄCHTOLD

Zumikon, created the colorful fashionable shoes. See also pp. 10/11, 92/93, 146 and 149.

MARTIN EBERHARD

born in 1949, lives in Kaiserstuhl. Following an apprenticeship in display design and time spent abroad in Israel, he worked as a script painter and graphic designer. Today, he works as a freelance illustrator, drawing to bring in the money and painting to feed his soul. His cow symbolizes the bookstore and gallery, "Buch und Kunst", decorated in hand-written text from Franz Hohler and spotted in colorful tones.

DÉDÉ MOSER

the most famous Swiss painter of cats, lives in Brione sopra Minusio, in the continuous company of cats and dogs. There, she has her work exhibited in a small gallery: oil paintings on canvas, paper, wood and metal covered in varnished paints, which bring about an impression of lightness and movement. In addition, etchings on copper and Plexiglas, as well as bronze sculptures attest to her diverse talents, which can also be seen in her life-size "Josephine" covered in cats.

Marcel Hohl, Bilder / Einrahmungen
location: Schaffhauserstrasse 24B/Berninaplatz

Sternen-Apotheke
location: Schaffhauserstrasse 350 / Sternen Oerlikon.

Buch und Kunst, Buchhandlung and Galerie Nievergelt
location: Franklinstrasse 23.

Schuhaus Walder AG, location: Edisonstrasse 10 / Welchogasse,
CSC Ploenzke IT-Services GmbH, location: Binzmühlestrasse 40.

OERLIKON'S MARKTPLATZ

MILKOVICS KALMAN

Zurich, is deaf. For over 10 years, he has been a sign maker and graphic designer for Köbi Möri Beschriftungen Zürich. In his free time, he paints and exhibits his work in various galleries. He has contributed six cows to this summer's event, the "Erdbeer-Mareieli" (Strawberry Girl) for the City Cafeteria. The "Hohl-Kuh" (Hollow Cow) is literally "in the picture" the frame dangling around her neck. Golden stars cover the Sternen-Apotheke. The "Z'Oerlike gits alles" cow is like puzzle-pieces which fit together. The "Schreinerin" (Carpenter) from Paul Kleger and another for Köbi Möri Beschriftungen are products of his creativity.

WERNER MARTI

Zurich, decorated the "Bijou".

Bijouterie Fiechter
location: Querstrasse 11 / Marktplatz.

Oerlikon's stylish Marktplatz has evolved over time into the main plaza for the whole region lying behind the Milchbuck – Züri-Nord – which includes about one quarter of the residents of Zurich.

A railway juncture since 1856, Oerlikon was the quickest among its neighboring country-side communities, Seebach and Affoltern, to develop urban features. The first signs of prosperity came in 1876 with the development behind the train station of the "Maschinenfabrik Oerlikon" MFO (Machine Factory Oerlikon). In 1896, Oerlikon built a single streetcar going into Zurich's city center, and eventually added branch lines that transported factory workers to Seebach and Dübendorf.

Long waged the war between the three farming neighbors and wealthy Oerlikon, until the city overtook the whole Glattal community. On the eve of their incorporation, the St. Niklaus Guild, out of which later came the Schwamendingen Guild, was founded, establishing its headquarters in Zurich.

Association "Z'Oerlike gits alles", location: Marktplatz.

Wanner Optik / Boutique. location: Welchogasse 4, Marktpkatz.

THE COW AND THE COLOSSEUM

HANS PETER STEINER

born in 1956, lives and works in Zurich-Oerlikon. The craftsman started out learning to paint auto-didactically. Various people along the way who discovered his talent, supported and promoted this former secondary school teacher. His expansive frescos and mosaics, his sculptures and statues, paintings and embroidery in every size and technique can be found spread out all over the world. He has managed to create his work without putting himself in the spotlight, instead finding support through friends and insiders who acquire his work.

The "Bergblumen-Kuh" (Mountain Flowers Cow) with the Asian touch, and the "ausgepresste Orange" (Squeezed Orange) are the fantastic creations of this artist. See p. 150.

At the first neighborhood movie house in Oerlikon, on Dreihkönigstag (Three Kings Day, celebrated on January 6) in 1912, the "most magnificent cinemato-graphic palace in Switzerland," advertised as the "most modern entertainment establishment", the "Kino-Theater Colosseum", opened its doors along the Zürcherstrasse in Oerlkon (today's Ohmstrasse). It showed the first of newsreel-like films from the first World War along with all kinds of adventure-pact silent films set to the music of its own house orchestra. Every Friday, there was a new program. This "Revolverchuchi" (a slang term used for movie houses showing plenty of shoot-outs) held out for sixty years before losing out to movie houses with better technology. Today, the only thing that remains as a reminder of Oerlikon's former pioneer movie theater is the old sign printed on the fassade.

Chäs-Bächler / Fehlmann Früchte und Gemüse
location: Welchogasse 4 / Schaffhauserstrasse.

IDEAL FOR BIKING

HANS PETER STEINER

Zurich, designed the "ausgepresste Orange" (Squeezed Orange). The orange is the logo for the Coop Bank. See also p. 150 and 154.

Oerlikon has always been very receptive to sports of all kinds, but most especially to bicycling. Many well-known bikers grew up here, and even a few veteran racers opened a bike shop here. Just outside the settlement, near the Tramstrasse, a public racing track opened in 1912, in the footsteps of the Biking Stadium Hardau, which had opened in 1812 only to close down again in the winter of 1905. The racing business in Oerlikon was also very dependent on weather conditions. But in 1938/39, an indoor stadium was erected, which served, alongside biking, mainly as an exhibition building and multi-purpose hall.

Coop Bank
location: Franklinstrasse 14.

AT THE GATE TO THE WORLD

BELDONA-DISPLAY TEAM

It took this team over 200 hours of work to cover their cow in mirrors; the result, a shimmering beauty.

KUONI DISPLAY TEAM

have created a real Swiss cow .

SANDRA BOSSHARD

Dielsdorf, decorated her Swiss lady with crispy cookies and sweet delicacies.

CORDULA HUBER

Zurich, created the day and night panoramas – see also pp. 72/73.

ALEX ZWAHLEN

Zurich, designed the dragon. See also pp. 14, 80/81, 88/89.

ASIA Coffee Shop
location: Terminal A.

Zurich's international revolving door – Kloten Airport – is now in its 50th year. It was back in June 1948, under the motto, "cosmopolitan Zurich", that the first runway was put into operation. By the mid-seventies the number of passengers had come to surpass the number of residents in all of Switzerland, and continues to climb to this day. For Zurich, this international gate way is tremendously advantageous to its livelihood. But for the residents in the outlying areas, the noise has reached its threshold. They are now demanding 100 million francs in compensation. Not the least bit phased, though, are the cows out grazing the airport plaza.

right page, Steiner Bäckerei-Konditorei AG, Zürich
location: Flughafen Terminal A.

Kuoni Business Travel AG, location: Terminal B.

UBS, location: Terminal A.
Beldona AG, location: Terminal A.

COLORFUL COWS – AS FAR AS THE EYE CAN SEE!

① **Silvia Isagro,** Krebsliga Kanton Zürich, for ZFV-Unternehmungen.

② **Kathy Moser,** DEFACTO, Zürich for Hotel Splügenschloss.

③ **Dekoteam Christ,** Zürich for Christ AG.

④ **Gertrud Arpagaus,** Zürich for Bernie's.

⑤ **Dekoteam Christ,** Zürich for Christ AG.

⑥ **F+F Farbe + Form,** Schule für Experimentelle Gestaltung, Zürich for Friemel Schuhmode.

⑦ **Dekoteam Kurz,** Zürich for JUWELIER KURZ.

⑧ **Heinz Blum,** Zürich for Hotel Rigihof.

⑨ **Joe Drobar,** Mining, for Nöggi.

⑩ Colored Passion, **Darko Kneze-vic, Phillip Käser,** Baden for Franz Carl Weber / Waro AG.

⑪ **Peter Pellanda,** Zürich for Boutique Marie Claire AG.

⑫ **Marcel Gerber,** Neunkirch, for The Pelican Drive, Staub Motos AG.

⑬ **Cia Coray,** Oberrieden **Urs Koller,** Rorschach for Chronometrie Beyer.

⑭ **Urs Leuenberger-Team,** Zürich for Behindertenwerk St. Jakob.

⑮ Jakob Rohner AG, Balgach.

⑯ **Kalman Milkovics,** Zürich for Schreinerei Paul Kleger AG.

⑰ Comité d'initiative Sion 2006, Sion, originally decorated with 5 Olympic rings, now spray-painted over.

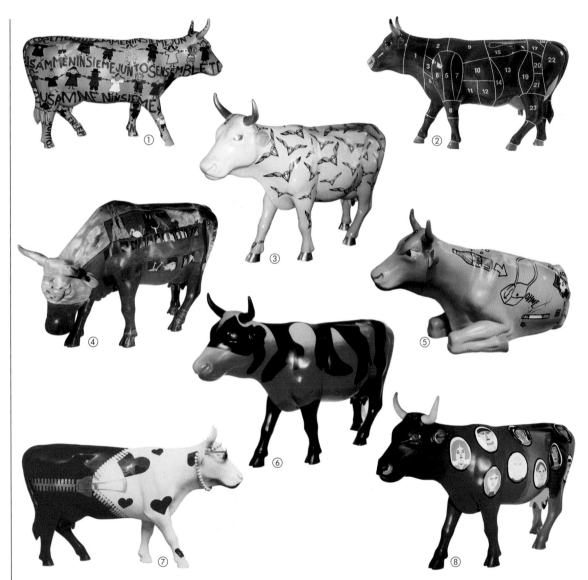

A SUCCESS STORY

THE PROJECT MANAGEMENT TEAM

Made up of the board members of the city association, three creative consultants and the director of the city association.

Rico Bisagno, Jelmoli SA
OK President

Robert Ober, Robert Ober AG
OK Deputy to the President

Dr. Rolf Baumgartner, UBS
Finances

Andreas Zürcher, Managing Director
of the City Association
OK Secretary and Legal Consultant

Roland Stahel, Zürich Tourismus
Foreign Promotion

Walter Knapp
Idea, Production, Creative Consultant

Beat Seeberger, EBSQU
Creative Consultant, Conceptualization, Realization

Martin Schorno
Sponsoring, Communications, Events, PR

It took two years to plan the "Cow Parade" and the organizers had to jump many hurdles to get to what today is a success story.

The Organizer

of the event is the over 1500-member City Association of Zurich, which was until June 1998 under the presidency of G. A. Marinello, Marinello AG, Zurich. Since then, Robert Ober, of Robert Ober AG, has been President.

Idea from Walter Knapp

His proposal to populate the city with painted cows was chosen as the best out of a series of suggestions put forth. At his request, the Atelier for Zoological Preparations, located in Näfels (GL), constructed a realistic scaled model which was received with enthusiasm – the plan was born.

From Model to Prototype

The next step was to go from the small model to three life-size cow models situated in different positions. The sculptor, Pascal Knapp from New York, was consulted. The artist, represented by Galierie Andy Illien, proved his artistic abilities with excellent prototypes. Lab technician, R. Müller, as well as the Cow Breeding Association, gave them a seal of approval, convincing the experts and artists, alike.

Production

All of the cows were produced in a variation of 3 types – standing, sitting and grazing – by the Hal-

Unpainted and painted cows at the warehouse Welti Furrer

lauer firm, "Klarer Freizeitanlagen AG". The objects are made of polyester resin and are hollow inside to reduce weight and save on material. The dimensions are 220 cm (length) x 65 cm (width) x 114 cm (height). The firm "Klarer" is a main sponsor of this event.

Cows, Artists, Costs

The 815 plain, unpainted cows went to 395 buyers at the cost of Fr. 1998 per cow. Approximately 400 artists, graphic designers and entire school classes were commissioned by the cow owners to paint the cows, bringing in an additional cost of about Fr. 1500–Fr. 3000 (depending on the artist) per cow.

Storage and transportation

It wasn't easy storing, loading, unloading and setting up 800 life-size cows. "Welti-Furrer", Zürich, the 2nd main sponsor of the event, which incidentally celebrates its 125th anniversary this year, managed the logistics at a minimal fee.

With the City's Blessing

Thanks to the city's government, Josef Estermann to be exact, the doors to many governmental departments were opened. Without the active support during the planning phase, as well as the handling of traffic during set-up, the approval of such a big event might never have been possible.

City Mayor Josef Estermann and President of the Zurich City Association, G.A. Marinello (left) at the press reception for the event's

COW INDEX

Hotel Montana, 8005 Zürich; 598; Konradstrasse 39
Hotel Schweizerhof, 8023 Zürich; 250; Bahnhofplatz 7; Marlies Zürcher/Andrea Brunner, DEFACTO, Zürich (S. 20–21)
Hotel Sofitel, 8035 Zürich; 75/76; Stampfenbachstrasse 60; Jan Leiser, Zürich (S. 148)
Hotel Splügenschloss, 8027 Zürich; 290/291; Splügenstrasse 2; Kathy Moser, DEFACTO, Zürich (S. 158)

Institut für Umweltwissenschaften, 8057 Zürich; 784; Winterthurerstrasse 190, Uni Zürich, Gebäude 13; Prisca Horstink/Katrin Hefti, Zürich
Intercontainer-Interfrigo (ICF) s.c., 4008 Basel; 786; Kuhmobile im Hauptbahnhof; Antonio Canarini, Gruner & Brenneisen AG, Basel (S. 12–13)
Interessengemeinschaft Pelikanplatz/Talacker/Sihlporte, 8023 Zürich; 484–487; Pelikanplatz (Rasendreieck), Le Boucher Corpaato, Fribourg (S. 66–67)
Interhome, 8048 Zürich; 339; Bahnhofplatz 7; Peter Klick, Zürich (S. 20)
Interio AG, 8957 Spreitenbach; 695–697; Rennweg 42; Dominique Münger, Zürich
ITA Institut für technische Ausbildung AG, 8057 Zürich; 468; Welchogasse

Jacob Rohner AG Balgach, 9436 Balgach; 393/394; vor Schild/vor Manor (bei McDonalds); (S. 159)
Jecklin Musikhaus, 8024 Zürich; 511/512; Rämistrasse 42 u. 30; Anja Lahusen, Zürich (S. 138)
Jelmoli AG, 8021 Zürich; 28–68; Seidengasse
Juwelier Kurz AG, 8001 Zürich; 527/528; Uraniastrasse 26; Thomas Jufer, Deco Factory, Stansstad (S. 158)

Kaufleuten Restaurants, 8001 Zürich; 70; Pelikanplatz, vor Restaurant; Le Bocher Corpaato, Fribourg
Kaufmann, Peter, 8123 Ebmatingen; 691; Ebmatingen
Kitch'n'cook AG, 8034 Zürich; 370–373; Werdemühleplatz, Kirchgasse/Schifflände; Christina Baumann, Zürich/Sereina Feuerstein-Bucher, Zürich (S. 40), Irene Attia, Zürich
Kleiner, Konditorei Bäckerei AG, 8048 Zürich; 510; Kuttelgasse; Lanoé Joëlle, Zürich
Koch Optik, 8001 Zürich; 173–177; Bahnhofstrasse 11; Walter Knapp, Stäfa (S. 106-107)
Kohler, Walter, 8302 Kloten; 753; Egetswil/Kloten Spielplatz
Konditorei/Café Gnädinger, 8042 Zürich; 513; Schaffhauserstrasse 57; Linda Charlotte Guipponi, Zürich
Konsum Verein Zürich, 8021 Zürich; 15–27; Einkaufszentrum Letzipark; Benno Schulthess, Widen/Hansjörg Känel, Zurzach/Iris Elsner, Bremgarten u. Team (S. 140–141)
Kordeuter, Restaurationbetriebe, 8022 Zürich; 338; Bleicherweg 7a; Silvie Rapold/Susanne Blum, Luzern
Kramer-Restauration betriebe, 8005 Zürich; 13; Marie-Christine Büchi-Jabiolle, Uitikon (S. 136)
Krause Senn AG, 8021 Zürich; 419; Badenerstrasse 33
Kronenhof Sigrist AG, 8046 Zürich; 711; Wehntalerstrasse 551; Sandra Häberli, Francoredia GmbH, Küsnacht
Kuoni Business Travel, 8037 Zürich; 647–651; 320, Flughafen Terminal A + B, Bahnhofstrasse/Paradeplatz, Bahnhofstrasse 52/Fraumünsterstrasse 29/Limatquai/Dörfli; Dekoteam, Zürich (S. 156)
Kuoni Reisen AG, 8010 Zürich; 312–319, 321–327; Flughafen/Bahnhofplatz/Bellevue/Oerlikon/Wiedikon; Dekoteam, Zürich (S. 26–27 u. 114)
KV Zürich, 8001 Zürich; 481; Pelikanstrasse 18, Kaufleuten-Gebäude; Donat Achermann, Donatelli Cartoons, Zürich

l'arco blu GmbH, 8002 Zürich; 592; Tessinerplatz 3; Petro Martini, Unterengstringen (S. 130–131)
La Serlas Zürich, 8001 Zürich; 351/352; Paradeplatz, Bahnhofstrasse 27/Paradeplatz; Jürg Bächtold, Zumikon/Norlando Pobre, St. Gallen (S. 92–98); Bettina Truninger, Zürich
Läckerli-Huus, 4142 Münchenstein; 470/471; Basel/Shop Ville, Zürich, Le Boucher Corpaato, Fribourg
Landolt Arbenz AG, 8001 Zürich; 739; Bahnhofstrasse 65; Brigitte Windlin, Zürich
Laredo, 8001 Zürich; 336; St. Peterstrasse 11
Leder-Locher AG, 8022 Zürich; 181–183; Bahnhofstrasse 91, Münsterhof 18; Gino Borradori, Dietikon Rahel Arnold, Zürich/Jan Leiser, Zürich (S. 118)
Lehner AG, 9050 Appenzell; 85; Bahnhofstrasse 48; Sylvia Bühler, Herisau
Leinenhaus Bogorad & Co., 8023 Zürich; 288; Usterstrasse, Löwenplatz; Brigitte Forrer/S. Peccora, Deko-Abteilung, Zürich (S. 36–37)
Les Ambassadeurs SA, 8001 Zürich; 298; Bahnhofstrasse 64; Cyrano Devanthey, Zürich

Leuthard, Rolf, Malergeschäft, 8114 Dänikon; 800/810; Seefeldquai 1; Frascati, Rolf Leuthard, Dänikon
Lindenmeyer, Dr. med. Ch., 8001 Zürich; 721; Wiese Rämipost; Isabelle Fallatz/Moritz Lindenmeyer, Zürich
Locher & Cie AG, 8022 Zürich; 509; Pelikan-Platz 5; Maler Schaub, Zürich (S. 68–69)
LOPARDO, 8001 Zürich; 501; Weinplatz 10, Limmat; Michael Heusi, Zürich/Atelier Aroma, Lukas Meier u. Team (S. 123)
Loretz Claudia, 4515 Oberdorf; 701; Hechtplatz/Limmatquai; Claudia Loretz, Oberdorf (S. 114)
Luftseilbahnen Saas-Fee, 3906 Saas-Fee; 787; Kuhmobile im Hauptbahnhof Zürich, (S. 12–13)

Madame, 8001 Zürich; 498/499; Bahnhofstrasse 63; Arthur Berini, Zürich (S. 32)
Manor AG, 8001 Zürich; 2–6; Bahnhofstrasse 75 u. Füsslistrasse; Deko-Team Manor, Zürich/Bruno Lauber, Zürich (S. 35)
Marbert Cosmetics, 8105 Watt; 410; Neben Pestalozziwiese; Kathy Moser, DEFACTO, Zürich (S. 35)
Märchenhotel Bellevue, 8784 Braunwald; 772; Limmatquai 54; Beat Andreas Brunner, Sculptura, St. Gallen
Marinello AG, 8023 Zürich; 662–664; Rathausbrücke, Flughafen Kloten; Ursula Dörig, Uster (S. 124–125) Eva Morell, Embrach
MARSANO AG, 8001 Zürich; 636; Paradeplatz; Jürg Bächtold, Zumikon/Norlando Pobre, St. Gallen (S. 92–98)
Mathis Food Affairs, 7500 St. Moritz; 133–134; Corviglia (Bergstation Drahtseilbahn)
Max Ditting AG, 8001 Zürich; 439/440; am Rennweg 35; Herr Rodriguez, Schweiz/Herr Sequillo, Equador
McDonald's, 1023 Crissier; 514–522; Pestalozziwiese, Bellevue/Central; Peter Sauter und Team, Atelier Fabritastika, Brüttisellen (S. 34–35)
Medienhaus Kloten, 8302 Kloten; 706–708; Limmatquai; Schule Opfikon
Meister Juwelier AG, 8001 Zürich; 329/330; Bahnhofstrasse 33; Alex Zwahlen, Zürich (S. 80–81)
Meister Silber AG, 8001 Zürich; 502–503; Bahnhofstrasse 28 a, Münsterhof 20; Alex Zwahlen, Zürich Heidi Mathis, Stallikon (S. 119)
Messer Dolmetsch, 8152 Glattbrugg; 186–189; Filialen Shop Ville/Limmatquai 126/Bahnhofstrasse 92; Heiri Sollberger, Zürich (S. 28)
Metzgerei Zgraggen, 8001 Zürich; 710; Hirschenplatz; Eppler Maler AG, Zürich
Michel Jordi SA, 1260 Nyon; 311; Bahnhofstrasse 48 u. 50; Heiko Cornelsen, Nyon (S. 74)
micro-electric Hörgeräte AG, 6301 Zug; 601/602; Schweizergasse 10; Gerhard Müller, Dietikon (S. 27) Suzanne Heiniger, Jonen
Mietervereinigung Shop Ville, 8023 Zürich; 86–95; Shop Ville alt (Bahnhofpassage); Andi Luzi, Neuhausen (S. 14–15)
Mietervereinigung Shop Ville, 8023 Zürich; 610–614; Abgänge ins Shop Ville Bahnhofpassage; Andi Luzi, Neuhausen (S. 14–15)
Mietervereinigung Zentrum Hauptbahnhof, 8023 Zürich; 193–212; Shop Ville, Hauptbahnhof (SBB-Areal) (S. 16–17)
Mietervereinigung Bahnhof Stadelhofen, 8023 Zürich; 215–234; Bhf-Stadelhofen/Stadelhofen Down Town (SBB-Areal); Nicola Condoleo, Opfikon/Reto Huber, Uetikon (S. 133–134)
Mietervereinigung Stadelhoferpassage, 8065 Zürich; 241/242; Stadelhoferpassage, Stadelhoferstrasse 22/28; Ursula Rutishauser, Feldmeilen/Peter Wiskemann/Kinder Malschule Zemp, Männedorf (S. 136)
Migros Genossenschafts-Bund, 8031 Zürich; 712; Am Guggenberg 22, Garten; W. Burth, Cactus, St. Gallen
Migros Zürich, 8005 Zürich; 446–465; Löwenplatz/Löwenstrasse 32, 29, 25, 11 u. 9; Dekorationsgestalter-Lehrlinge, Migros Zürich (S. 36–39)
Milchverband St.Gallen–Appenzell, 9201 Gossau (SG); 377; Pelikanplatz; Kundry/Hans Niederhauser, Fruthwilen (S. 64–65)
Möbel Pfister AG, 5034 Suhr; 281–285; Neumühlequai 10/12, Walcheplatz; Emilie Frey/Tony de Giorgi/Sybille Hediger/Alex Mondracchia-Boxhoorn/Nicole Perrin/Deko-TeamMöbel Pfister, Zürich
Moda-Parade, 8001 Zürich; 272; Bahnhofstrasse 24; Patricia Grieder, Zumikon
Modehaus Gassmann AG, 8001 Zürich; 178–180, 637; Poststrasse 5/7; Gassmann-Deko-Team, Zürich (S. 100–101), Jürg Bächtold, Zumikon/Norlando Pobre, St. Gallen (S. 92–98)
Modehaus Goldschmidt, 8023 Zürich; 581; Bahnhofstrasse 65
Modehaus Krause Senn AG, 8004 Zürich; 568; Badenerstrasse 44
modissa AG, 8021 Zürich; 340–344; Bahnhofstrasse 73 u. 74
Mohn & Partner AG, 8154 Oberglatt; 751; Geissbühlstrasse 26, 8353 Elgg
Moos, Giuliani, Hermann Architekten, 8253 Diessenhofen; 184; Selnaustrasse 2 (Unique-Travel); Christoph Steinemann, Ennetbaden
Möri Köbi, Beschriftung und Siebdrucke, 8051 Zürich; 720; Luegislandstrasse 137; Milkovics Kalman, Zürich

Bibliography

DER BUND, Bern, 30. Juni 1998	54
Alfred Hauser, Was für ein Leben – Schweizer Alltag vom 15. bis 18. Jahrhundert, Verlag NZZ, Zürich	102
Beat Krenger, BLICK, Zürich, 25. Mai 1998	66
Gerold Meyer von Knonau, Historisch-geographisch-statistisches Gemälde der Schweiz, Zürich, 1844	136
Dr. B. Schmeil, Leitfaden der Tierkunde, Leipzig 1933. 150. Auflage	50
Stuttgarter Zeitung, Stuttgart, 27. Mai 1998	86
Tages-Anzeiger, Leserbriefe, 4. Juni 1998	126
Zürichdeutsches Wörterbuch, 1983	28
Zürichsee-Zeitung, Stäfa, 22. April 1998	68

Photograph Credits

Aerial photo: swissphoto vermessung ag, 8105 Regensdorf-Watt	9
Bank Julius Bär AG, 8001 Zürich	84, 85
Behindertenheim St. Jakob, 8005 Zürich	159
Christ, 8037 Zürich	158
Coop Bank, 8050 Zürich	155
The Fabergé Imperial Easter Eggs, Christies Books, Christie, Manson and Woods Ltd., 1997	89
EBSQU, Beat Seeberger, 8005 Zürich,	7, 14/15, 16/17, 121, 159, 161
Fritzsche, Charly, Quartier-Echo, 8032 Zürich	140/146
Galerie Commercio, 8001 Zürich	132
Galerie Ernst Hohl, 8001 Zürich	82
Galerie Nievergelt, 8050 Zürich	151
Genossenschaft Migros, 8031 Zürich	38/39
Klick, Peter, 8034 Zürich	20
Köbi Möri, 8051 Zürich	151
Konsum Verein Zürich, 8021 Zürich	140/141
Kurz Juwelier, 8001 Zürich	158
Lokal-Info Zürichberg, Ch. P. Zufal, 8703 Erlenbach	7
St. Annahof, 8001 Zürich	62
Schorno Marketing, Martin Schorno, 8005 Zürich	27, 48, 60, 94/95, 122, 138, 148/149, 158
Schmid, Christof, 8810 Horgen	116
Dr. P. Schnötzinger, 8053 Zürich	151
Schuhhaus Walder, 8050 Zürich	151
Sportbahnen Elm, 8767 Elm	12
Steiner, Hans Peter, 8050 Zürich	154
Weber, Hans Rudolf, 8127 Forch	59
ZFV-Unternehmungen, 8001 Zürich	158
Zwahlen, Alex, 8005 Zürich	156
Zürcher Kantonalbank, 8600 Dübendorf	108

Land in Sicht
Auf nach Zürich!

Bekannte Dichter,
berühmte Leute,
Sie kamen nach Zürich,
sprachen und speisten,
besser oder schlechter,
heiter und satirisch,
damals und heute.

Vera de Bluë
Werner Hausmann

In und um die Öpfelchammer

ISBN 3-85820-092-1
Fr. 19.80

NEPTUN VERLAG AG, Postfach, CH-8280 Kreuzlingen
Telefon 071 664 20 20 · Fax 071 664 20 23